AUTHOR'S INTRODUCTION

In this latest of my many books about the Blackpool Tramway I have decided to concentrate on the tram fleet in the post-war years, and see whether our fleet today is the best we could have had. Depending on your age and experience of our trams, as readers you will form an opinion as I have done. However, I hope that you will also enjoy reading about my experience as a conductor of Coronation cars in 1964, and also about all the tours which have been held since 1939, complete with memorable events. Undoubtedly the Coastal Tramway has provided Blackpool with one of its famous attractions, along with the Tower, Pleasure Beach and Illuminations. I am sure that you – like me – are looking forward to the 125th Anniversary of the Promenade Tramway in 2010. I hope we will see Conduit-car 4 leading a twenty-tram procession again!

Don't Forget – Cars Stop By Request,
STEVE PALMER

FOREWORD

The Blackpool Tramway is, amongst other things, a great survivor – as is demonstrated by its 121 year's of history. Over the decades there have been many crises and problems, but the tramway and its long line of Managers have risen to these challenges, made difficult decisions, and ensured the continuation of this unique transport system and icon of the north's, if not the nation's, socio-economic history.

In 2007 the signs for the long-term future of the Tramway are encouraging. In the last five years Blackpool Transport has achieved three record profit years and enjoyed five of its seven most successfull years ever. 2006/2007 will be the Company's most profitable year to date due to the continued growth of the Metro Coastlines bus network, the new improved concessionary fares arrangements for senior citizens and the elderly, and a reduction in the Tramway's losses during the out of season and early season periods.

These improved profits have enabled Blackpool Transport to provide the Council with over £5 million in dividend and track rental payments in the last few years to fund essential track upgrading and to start to address years of under-investment. On top of this Blackpool Borough Council's successful bid for £10.7 million of funding from central Government for the renewal of the electrical Sub-Station in Copse Road in the winters of 2006/2007 and 2007/2008, will by the summer of 2008 provide Blackpool's trams with the best infrastructure that they have had to run on in years.

Much more funding and work is still required before the whole of the system is brought up to appropriately modern standards, and Blackpool and Lancashire Councils are still awaiting a green light from Government for the full Tramway Upgrade Scheme and new low-floor trams in particular.

The recent rejection of Blackpool Borough Council's Super Casino bid has also been a blow to the Fylde Coast's morale. Having said all that, the portents for the future of the tramway look better now than at any time in the last ten years, and we can look forward to 2010 and the 125th Anniversary of the Tramway with great hope.

Steve Palmer's excellent new book on Blackpool Transport's trams provides a fascinating insight into the wonderful range of vehicles which have served generations of visitors to Blackpool and locals alike. This new book is written with great affection and once again demonstrates Steve Palmer's considerable knowledge of the Blackpool Tramway and its much-loved trams. I would strongly recommend Blackpool Trams – Past and Present to anyone with an interest in the Blackpool system, its vehicles and transport in general.

Steve Burd
Managing Director
27th March 2007

BLACKPOOL'S TRAMS

PAST & PRESENT

BY

STEVE PALMER

Venture *publications*

DESIGN AND COMPUTER ORIGINATION: JOHN A SENIOR

Trade Distribution and Sales Enquiries
MDS Booksales 128, Pikes Lane Glossop Derbyshire
SK13 8EH 01457 861508
www.venturepublications.co.uk
email   info@venturepublications.co.uk

Almost half a century separates these two images of illuminated trams in Blackpool.
Below is the famous Progress Car, seen in 1957, and opposite a view in 2005 showing
Fisherman's Friend and HMS Blackpool passing on the Promenade. *(JA Senior both)*

CONTENTS

The Tram Fleet Today

Looking back over 50 years of the Blackpool tramway raises questions about the fleet today. Fifty years ago the fleet consisted of 159 trams; now there are 46 trams available for service and 29 stored for optional further use. The post-war tram fleet of 159 trams eventually comprised 116 of the 'thirties streamliners, 8 Standards, 10 Pantograph cars and 25 new Coronations. Undoubtedly Walter Luff's time, 1933-54, has to be identified as the strongest successful era, clearly because the popular seaside resort required a strong fleet of trams providing a frequent service on four routes. The streamlined fleet of the 'thirties comprised 65 Railcoaches, 12 open Boat cars, 27 double-deckers and 12 sun saloons, replacing previous generations of Promenade open-top cars and crossbench and saloon cars of the Tramroad Company. Walter Luff always stated that the value of the Railcoaches was created in their swift and attractive facilities for the public – with cushioned seats, opening windows, sunshine sliding roofs, electric clocks, and heaters for the cold weather – meeting the challenge of the Standards, until the system was modernised in post-war years. The Balloon saloon cars were primarily used on the Squires Gate route, while the open-toppers and Boat cars were featured on the Promenade, where the thousands of visitors enjoyed riding on them. The Pantograph cars of the 'twenties were exclusively used on the North Station-Fleetwood route in the summer season, while the eight Standards were seen as useful 'specials' on the Promenade between Cabin and Harrowside. With 78 seats they were more economical using a driver and conductor rather than the crew of three on Balloon-cars.

Top: Representative fleet line-up at North Pier in the 'fifties; notice the Balloon in green livery and the typical centre-entrance Burlingham bus coming out of Talbot Square.

Left: The famous Marton route terminus at Royal Oak, with Vambac 21 about to return using the trolley-reverser – hence the passengers facing the other way.

Facing page: An interesting trio of trams – Coronation 328, Railcoach 201 and Twin-car 275-T5 at Fleetwood Ferry, of which only the renumbered twin set 675-685 remain in existence today. (John Fozard, all)

However, the developments in the post-war years of Walter Luff did feature the modernisation of the Marton route, which he saved by waging a campaign to show its great value, both for residents and holidaymakers who could ride from Talbot Square or South Pier to Stanley Park. As it was relaid in 1948, he intended that modern cars would be used, following the USA example of successful President's Conference Cars (PCCs) in the 'thirties. It is known that manufacturers of tramway equipment in Britain acquired a TRC licence to build PCC cars – but in essence Crompton Parkinson created British-made equipment known as 'VAMBAC' (Variable Automatic Multi-notch Braking & Acceleration Control). In Britain there was great interest in PCC development during post-war years by Liverpool, Leeds and Glasgow, but owing to the immediate demise of the Liverpool system, only Leeds and Glasgow acquired Vambac demonstrators – numbered 602 and 1005 respectively. Accordingly, 41 Vambac cars were produced, 39 of which were Blackpool cars – 208 and 303 as demonstrators, Sun saloons 10-21 of 1939, and 25 new Coronation cars. The Maley & Taunton bogies used under these Vambac cars were every bit as quiet as PCC cars. Maley & Taunton was licensed by Clark Equipment Company to build trucks from its designs which formed the basis of their HS-44 bogies in Britain. In Blackpool a total of 43 sets of bogies were obtained, 18 for Marton cars and 25 for Promenade cars. Apart from the Coronations, fourteen were used, including Brush car 303 which remained at Bispham depot owing to its trials on Marton highlighting problems of slow sliding doors. The four sets of bogies remained in Blundell Street depot as 'spares', although they should have been fitted to Marton Railcoaches. The Coronation cars became Walter Luff's crowning glory before his retirement in 1954. However, subsequently it was found that they became expensive liabilities, and by 1975 were scrapped with the implication that they had been a disadvantage to the survival of the Tramway. Also, the Marton Vambac cars, including the demonstrators 208 and 303, were broken up in 1963, except for the survival of 11 which has recently been restored at East Anglia Transport Museum. Three Vambac cars thus remain in Britain, Marton Vambac 11, Leeds 602 at Crich and 304 at Blackpool, showing how smooth and silent a British version of the American PCC can be.

However, putting the nails in the Coronation's coffin began in 1964, as 313 had the Vambac equipment removed, and thereby creating a spare pair of bogies. It was stored on trestles in Bispham Depot until it made its final exit in January 1966 towed by Works car 5, and became the first Coronation to be scrapped in 1968. The first service-tram to lose Vambac equipment was 323 in 1964, and was fitted with the EE Z6 controllers. My own experience as a conductor found 323 a slow operator, lacking the swift acceleration of the Vambac equipment. However, it was decided to proceed with twelve Coronations to be refitted with conventional equipment, and they were repainted in the new half green and cream livery with an orange trolley tower. It was intended that they could maintain the Fleetwood route as service cars, and that the remaining twelve Vambac Coronation cars could be scrapped, retaining 304 for preservation at the National Tramway Museum. Scrapping started in 1969 at Thornton Gate siding, where the dismantled Coronation cars were passed by others still in service! Owing to public objection to the burning of these trams, the remaining Coronation Vambac cars were quietly broken up in Blundell Street depot, away from the public view.

By 1971 only nine Coronations were still in seasonal use, and in 1974 660 was selected for preservation in the fleet, and fully overhauled as a representative of the class. By 1975 the final season arrived for the Coronations, when five of them clattered along the Promenade as specials, after which they were withdrawn. Number 304 by this time was stored at Clay Cross store, subsequently at Burtonwood and St Helens, having been rejected by the National Tramway Museum (NTM) who already owned Leeds 602 as a Vambac. Of the final five, 663 was surprisingly bought by 17 year old Graham Oliver – a self-confessed 'tram maniac' – and it first went to the Steam Centre at Lytham, subsequently to Southport Steam Museum and Bradford Transport Museum, and is today stored in Marton by the Lancastrian Transport Trust (LTT). The introduction of the OMO cars can clearly be seen as a more economic replacement for the Coronations, albeit making a false start with Brush car 638 in 1969. One-man operation was seen as a saviour for the Blackpool & Fleetwood coastal line, since the Department of Transport was offering 50% grants towards the costs of new one-man buses. Manager JC Franklin succeeded in getting a grant for the proposed trams, so a planning committee was formed by Blackpool Transport and succeeded in producing a new generation of trams for the existing fleet. The source of these OMOs had to be the thirteen remaining English Electric Railcoaches, including three first series and ten second series cars. Although listed with the 30 cars for rebuilding, the Brush cars proved not to be suitable for an extension of the body and thus remained as conventional Railcoaches. It is true that while OMOs became very useful, their extended bodies became bent because the bogie mounting should have been repositioned. They were ultimately replaced by eight Centenary cars beginning with 641 in 1984. There should have been ten, but two Jubilee double-deckers had previously been completed as OPOs. Of the thirteen OMOs, ten were broken up and three survived: numbers 5 in store at NTM Clay Cross, 8 owned by LTT at Blackpool, and although number 10 became a cafe near Reading, in 2005 it was dismantled providing spares for number 8!

In 2005, it had been considered that the Blackpool fleet of 75 trams was too large in proportion to the reduction of day visitors, down from 7.1 million in 1987 to 3.9m in 2003, and staying visitors from 16m to 10.3m in the same years. In response to this the operating fleet has been reduced to 46 cars, leaving 29 withdrawn including four Boats in reserve. Looking at the situation today, the fleet comprises 20 Balloons, 10 OPO cars 641-648, 761 and 762, five Twin-cars 671 and 681 – 675 and 685, five Railcoaches 626, 630, 631, 678, 680, four historic cars 40, 66, 147, 660 and illuminated cars Cevic trawler 633 and Frigate 736. From this selection of remaining trams, the question is raised as to which survivors of the original fleet of 159 cars are the right ones? In contrast to the loss of the Coronations, survival of the double-deck Balloons – as the largest class of the 'thirties streamliners – supplied useful capacity on the coastal route. This has evolved from their introduction to Fleetwood in 1958, first used on the summer service in 1972 and subsequently so used in recent years.

Coronations 304 & 660 together on tour at Rossall Lane in May 2005, recreating a familiar scene of the Fleetwood and Starr Gate service 35 years before. Renumbering of the fleet took place in 1968, shortly before withdrawals of these cars began. They were allocated numbers 641-64, having originally been 304-28, the missing number being that of 313 which was withdrawn after a long period out of service and without being renumbered. (See the fleet list at the rear of this book.) *(RP Fergusson)*

Undoubtedly the most handsome of the 'thirties streamliners, these trams became the Marton Vambacs in their post-war reincarnation. Here 11 is seen at Carlton Colville East Anglia Transport Museum as restored in 2005. *(Author)*

It is also interesting that the little-used Twin-cars gained in value during 2003, when they were introduced to the Starr Gate and Fleetwood route in the absence of the double-deckers, which were banned during track relaying. In retrospect, credit must go to JC Franklin, who perceived the Balloons as valuable service cars and also introduced the new Twin-cars in 1960. The recent use of four Boat cars in 2005 proved that they were still popular with the public, both along the Promenade and to Fleetwood on Market Days. The post-war survivors – Coronations 304 and 660 – look handsome and are able to effectively operate, 304 with reconstructed Vambac equipment by Bowers of Derby. Certainly, when a Coronation appears on the Promenade at Blackpool, it does attract the attention of the public, since it undoubtedly looks superior to the other trams. While we have to accept the demise of the 39 Vambac cars, there was every reason to have retained the ten Coronations with conventional equipment, and with the value of being able to carry more passengers. Of the modern fleet represented by the Centenaries, it is pleasing that they have been rebuilt and look much smarter in profile than they did originally. However, while operating the winter service they can be unreliable with their brakes fixed on until the engineering staff come and release them! Of course, this arises from their lack of emergency brakes as fitted to the conventional cars, albeit 70 years old.

So what of the future? Blackpool has applied to the Department of Transport for a grant of £88 million, with the support of the North West Regional Assembly. Their list of Priority Projects has included Blackpool in this region, since its tramway is the oldest operator in the UK, and its survival depends upon modernising for the 21st Century. It is deemed that there is a need for 15 articulated cars – possibly Skoda Astra – relaying the track in addition to recent improvements, and the renewal of the overhead from Thornton Gate to Fleetwood, together with new sub-stations and traction poles. It is also proposed that new platforms to match the low-floor trams, with level access, are to be fitted at the new 40 stops – reduced from 60 – in order to speed up the service and facilitate simultaneous loading and unloading. A new depot is proposed for the fleet, on the site of the former historic Blundell Street depot which was demolished in 1982. It is also planned that the maintenance shops should be re-designed and positioned, in order to provide easier access, rather than the present procedure of shunting trams across the bus parking yard. Apart from new trams for the inter-urban service, it is clear that some of the present fleet is to be retained to provide Promenade 'specials' at the height of the season and especially during the Illuminations. Regarding the legislation for easy access for the disabled in wheelchairs, it is hoped that Blackpool will be identified as a special case using historic vintage trams, along with the modern trams on a regular service facilitating their access. It is, therefore, hoped that Blackpool will continue operating its famous tramway as one of the popular attractions of the seaside resort. Thus, it will be interesting for us now to explore the evolution of the post-war fleet in the 20th century, along with restoration of historic trams and many tours for their fans.

The striking Blackpool 'Always Welcome' arch in 1954, framing Coronation 328 in service for Fleetwood, its trolley fitted with a swivel head. *(The Gazette)*

Marton Vambacs

Undoubtedly, the success of Walter Luff's *Five Year Plan 1933-1938*, with the introduction of 116 streamliner trams, provided Blackpool with an efficient fleet and leaving the Standards on the Marton route, representing the traditional British trams. It was planned to introduce fifteen smaller 72-seat versions of the double-decker Balloons to the Marton route, thus completing the modern fleet. The outbreak of war in September 1939 caused the cessation of such developments, and modernisation was deferred until the post-war years. The English Electric factory at Preston began manufacturing aircraft, but the final trams to be made there were four streamliners for Aberdeen, although they were assembled in the present GEC works. As far as the fleet of streamliners was concerned, they were reduced from their modern appearance by the predominantly green livery with cream flares at each end. Fender ends and centre buffers were painted white, to make trams more prominent in the darkened streets, while the headlamps were hooded. To conceal tram saloons from above, the curved roof windows were painted green and each saloon had only one boxed light. Riding on the trams in those war years must have changed the nature of their usage, since the population of Blackpool had increased by the arrival of thousands of servicemen for training, civil servants using the Norbreck Hydro hotel and others as offices, together with the Vickers Armstrong factory at Squires Gate building Wellington bombers. Patronage increased, and consequently the open-top double-deckers 237-49 were rebuilt as enclosed double-deckers with EE fittings by Blackpool Transport Works. Today represented by No. 700 in the wartime livery, it will be clear that these cars had a fixed roof but their top-deck seats were spartan, being wooden and upholstered by moquette. The double-deckers were used on the busy Squires Gate route throughout the year, but had one conductor in the early mornings.

The pressures of the War had resulted in the acquisition of Marton Depot by RAF Technical Training Command in November 1939, and the Standards were transferred to operate from Blundell Street depot. Bispham Depot was re-opened in 1940 to diversify the operating fleet, and the ten Pantograph cars returned with the 20 Brush cars for the first time. The Lytham St Annes bus garage on Squires Gate Lane was re-wired over four existing tracks for use by Blackpool Transport if required. The most modern streamliners, sun saloons 10-21 were used daily as 'range specials' for troops from South Promenade to Rossall, where they were trained on the rifle range of the public school. To compensate for delays caused for the Fleetwood service cars while the 'specials' unloaded ammunition boxes, rifles and troops, in July 1940 a siding was built to take six trams standing clear of the route. While it is now removed, the wider site exists next to the tram lines. The troops found the trams uncomfortable, and called them 'cattle-trucks', but in 1941 they were fitted with a fixed roof, winding windows and full length platform doors. Also, a partition was fitted to keep the driver – including women drivers – separate from the troops. Another scheme was planned to extend the line from Lytham Road terminus along Squires Gate Lane, to serve the Vickers Armstrong factory employees, but this did not materialise due to the lack of the required funding. VE Day at the end of the war came as a great relief to Blackpool, and was celebrated by the touring of the tram routes by the decorated Bandwagon car; flags were also hung from the trams' trolleys. A new post-war era enabled tramway development to resume, and there were even rumours of 'silent trams' for the Marton route!

Incidentally, the Air Ministry informed the Corporation that Marton depot would be derequisitioned at the beginning of 1945, thus the depot was restored for use in being re-wired for the return of the Standards and the Boat cars. Incidentally, there is evidence to suggest that Walter Luff's opinions changed over the years, seen in the report he made to the Transport Committee in December 1943, concerning the possible formation of regional transport boards after the war. He even made a proposal that trolleybuses could be used on the Marton route, with 25 of them serving a group of routes based on Marton Depot. In the same report, evidence of his pragmatic policies for trams still remained, proposing the purchase of 30 new trams and using £100,000 for track renewal after the war. His policy was still 'trams where the crowds are greatest', so his suggestions included extension of the South Promenade line to St Annes, incorporating a reserved track tramway. Such ambitious schemes today may seem fantastic, but they were in keeping with his view of the Fleetwood route: "There is no known system of transport that could give better public service, or better moving crowds results". Further improvements included the diversion of the Promenade track to the seaward-side of the Metropole Hotel in order to remove the traffic bottleneck, and improvement to rolling stock by the incorporation of 'certain PCC features'. His 'Post War Plan' would have cost £805,000 and given a 'super transport system', including tram usage being radio-controlled from the Transport Office.

It is interesting that the influence of the USA and PCC cars began to influence Britain, beginning in 1937 when Leeds Transport Manager W Vane-Morland acquired blueprints of the PCC cars, after viewing the Boston demonstrator. In fact, Leeds did not acquire its two experimental modern cars – 602 fitted with

Standard 159 showing LAYTON on its indicators at the entrance to Marton Depot, the latter surmounted by the Municipal coat-of-arms. All the Boats are out on the Promenade but just visible is a Pantograph visiting on a tour in 1959. *(RP Fergusson)*

Vambac equipment – until 1953. In 1944 the Liverpool Transport Manager Walter Marks issued a post-war planning report that called for a fleet of 750 PCCs, but in 1946 the City Council decided to replace the magnificent tramway system by a fleet of buses. Blackpool was involved in a committee of British tramway operators who were interested in operating PCC-type cars on their systems. At the end of the war, English Electric was approached by the American manufacturers to undertake making PCCs under licence for this country. Initially, the company declared the need for making at least 1,000 trams to justify their manufacture. However, there was mixed response because the design and size of the PCCs went against British double-deck tradition. The English Electric Company then proceeded with the manufacture of military aircraft instead. Nevertheless, Blackpool's Walter Luff still considered the future development of PCC-type cars was relevant to the future successful tramway operation. In 1946, his first priority was the modernisation of the Marton route, its necessary relaying and operation by modern trams, rather than having the smaller double-deckers of 1939. The 'Battle for Marton trams' started in January 1946, when Walter Luff and the Borough Surveyor presented their report on track renewal and alternative forms of transportation.

Initially the Transport Committee refused to make a decision and instructed the Surveyor to repair the track for a few years. The local press on 2nd February opened its campaign with the headlines 'TRAMS, BUSES OR TROLLEYBUSES FOR MARTON?' and supplied the comparative figures for each form of transport. To relay the track and equip the Marton route with new trams for would cost £136,380. Trolleybuses were the dearer choice at £148,000 for 20 trolleybuses, new substation and overhead wiring, whereas 20 buses were the cheapest option at £86,940 including resurfacing the road. Walter Luff indicated that he advocated the retention of the tramcars, and in their defence said that they could turn back in their own length, use home produced electricity, and could be fitted with resilient wheels and maintain a high average speed. As an added bonus, he pointed out that the retention of trams on the Marton route would make the continued Circular Tour possible. Here, for the first time, the virtue of the new PCC equipment was included in the argument for the retention of trams, and Walter Luff had to promote the great virtues of the 'silent trams'. The press continued its support for the Marton trams, reflecting the public opinion of the period. Councillor RW Marshall said: "We never have carried the same number of people by bus in Central Drive as we did by tram until 1936. Can anyone imagine how Blackpool could have carried on during the six war years without its tramways?"

With the continued delay in decision by the Council, Walter Luff found the chance he had been waiting for. He stated: "A tram, which by its sheer frequency and riding qualities, could compete with not just the bus, but with its future competitor the private car." In March 1946, the new Maley & Taunton resilient wheel bogies arrived in Blackpool, as a means of proving his argument. Two sets of bogies were supplied by Maley & Taunton, one pair of non-conventional type with spoked steel wheels and worm-gear drive, and the other with resilient wheels and spiral-bevel drive. Both had 6ft wheelbase and were inside-framed, allowing easy access to the wheels. As mentioned earlier Maley & Taunton were licenced by Clark Equipment

A view inside Marton depot early in 1958 showing 147 and 40 heading two lines of fourteen Standards, prior to six of them being taken to Thornton Gate before Easter, and broken up. *(Author)*

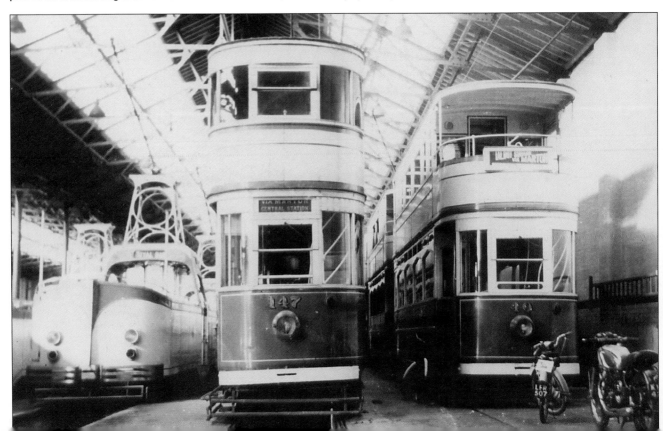

A post-war view of Rigby Road Depot, with cars in the green wartime livery, apart from sun saloons 10-21 retaining 1939 livery but with wartime rebuilding features evident. *(CE Box)*

Company of USA to build trucks from its designs for the PCC cars, hence the design of the M & T HS-44 bogies. The resilient wheels incorporated a rubber 'sandwich' between the hub and the tyre, which would effectively absorb vibrations of the kind made by corrugations, and thus give silent running. The M & T bogie featured a large reversed leaf-spring supporting the centre bolster, and heavy end brackets to carry the air brakes. Thus the new bogies lacked their compactness of their American counterparts, being necessarily fitted with discs on the outside of the wheels on which to apply the brake shoes by compressed air. The bogies also included magnetic track brakes with a long shoe suspended between the wheels. The chosen car for trials with the new M & T bogies was 1937 Brush car 303, and so it was repainted in a new livery of cream panels with green flares on the sides and V-flashes on the ends, thus providing the streamlined appearance. At 23.00 on 9th April, 303 went to the Marton route and after the service cars finished, ran over the worst track of the route. The press described it as 'sensational', and the BBC made recordings to compare the silence of 303 with the noise of the Standard cars on the worn track of the Marton route. All this publicity was excellent in the tramway case for the 'Battle for Marton'.

In preparation for the Crompton Parkinson Vambac control equipment due in November, 208 was prepared so that with 303 there would be two representative trams, each with different types of Maley & Taunton bogies. As in the case of 303, the position of the bolster was moved to accommodate the new 6ft wheelbase bogies, and the EE Z6 controllers were removed from the driver's cabs. A special chamber was built in the base of the trolley tower to contain the rotary converter unit, and the car was given a distinctive appearance by altering the front windscreens to include a pair of smoked-glass sunshields, since the driver would have to sit at the controls. Number 303 was lifted on 12th November and its resilient bogies were replaced by the M & T steel wheel set, 208 receiving the resilient-wheel bogies on the same day. Into the cabs of 208 was placed the remote-controller in a casing on the floor, over which the driver was to sit and beside this was the

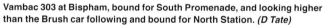

Vambac 303 at Bispham, bound for South Promenade, and looking higher than the Brush car following and bound for North Station. *(D Tate)*

11

tall contactor box. In the roof chamber the rotary accelerator unit was fitted and connected by cables to the controller in the cabs. Circular in shape, the resistances were arranged in a rotary bank with spring loaded fingers on the inside to make contact with them. To move these fingers, a rotary arm driven by a pilot motor moved round the circle attracting the fingers towards it with a permanent magnet, thus removing resistances by degrees. Although 90 steps are provided, 94 fingers were fitted, so that there was a permanent overlap of three contacts at all times. This unit was used for both accelerating and decelerating, and the movement of the rotary arm was determined by the forward thrust of the control stick or its pull back. The equipment was variable by the driver and yet automatic to ensure a smooth glide away, avoiding all jerkiness of the conventional controller. Number 208 retained its air braking equipment, adjusted to apply on to the outer braking drums of the HS-44 bogie. With all the wiring connected and the wooden panelling replaced, on 16th November 1946 all was ready for 208's first movement from the depot. All Corporation and Crompton Parkinson eyes were trained on the car as the controller arm was pushed forward by the driver for the first time. However, something went wrong, and in fact 208 refused to move. Hurriedly, the wiring diagrams were brought out and carefully examined by the electricians. A joiner removed the saloon panelling and electricians checked the wiring circuits, then the car moved forward as the first British car with similar PCC equipment. On the following night there was a trial run to Little Bispham, while on the 19th November 208 made its first contact with the well worn rails of the Marton route. Once it was established that all was well, the car was hastily repainted in the new cream livery in Blundell Street depot. Thus, 208's completion was not a moment too soon to impress the Town Council as a tram of the future for the Marton route.

A special meeting was held by the Transport Committee in November, 'to consider the form of transport for Marton, and that the Transport Manager be instructed to present a report on the matter to the meeting'.

A Railcoach in the attractive post-war livery, similar to the Brush cars in pre-war years and afterwards. *(John Fozard)*

A profile of 208 with Maley & Taunton bogies fitted with track brakes. Inside the tower is the Vambac equipment in a cream dome, whilst the saloon boasts the fluorescent lights. *(Author's Collection)*

Things had reached a critical stage, and the speed of the venerable Standards on the route had to be reduced, because of the shocking state of the track during December 1946. The Evening Gazette said: "The Council cannot much longer escape a decision on the future of this route. The tram is such an efficient means of transport and their retention would be in line with modern ideas, so their expense would be justified." Clearly, the impression made by 208's demonstration had made an impression! All this pressure had its effect upon the Transport Committee, when at the December meeting they heard from the Borough Surveyor that the track on the Marton route "was in too bad condition to be used for much longer, and either renewal or abandonment should be decided upon forthwith". Walter Luff also contributed his opinion, and fortunately it was decided that it should be recommended to the Council that the Marton tramway should be retained and the Surveyor instructed to proceed with the relaying of the track. The final act in the Marton drama took place on 8th January 1947, when the Town Council approved the Marton track-renewal by 25 votes to 21. The narrow majority in favour of retention indicated Walter Luff's success in tipping the voting-balance by demonstrating the experimental silent tramcar in 1946!

Provision was to be made during relaying for the clearance of 8ft wide cars over the service, showing that Mr Luff cherished the idea of completely new trams for Marton. However, rising costs should have made it obvious that his estimate of £5,000 each for new cars was by this time totally unrealistic. It was estimated that the relaying would take about a year and that 962 tons of rail would be needed, of which 300 tons was already in stock. The alacrity with which the Surveyor began the track renewal indicated the urgency of the situation, and in the week following the Council decision, the relaying started between Raikes Parade and Devonshire Square. So that the three-minute service could be maintained, single-line working was operated using a single-line staff between crossovers. The fact that the cars on the Marton route were fitted with swivel head trolleys enabled them to travel along the normal running wire, and saved a lot of delay in trolley-poling. At the next Transport Committee it was proposed that Thermit welding the rail-joints be adopted. In this way the ends of the street-rails were fused together to form continuous-rail throughout the route. This would add £350 to the Marton track bill, but upon the advice of Mr Luff, the Committee agreed. Only the very best would do for Marton, and Walter Luff was planning a tram service par excellence!

Some indication of the capital costs undertaken for the town's transport at this period were given by the figure of £300,000 to be spent on new trams and buses and £111,000 on track renewals. In 1946 tenders had been accepted from Leyland and Burlingham for the construction of 50 new buses, which were to be delivered in 1948. These would replace the pre-war buses and feature new elements in their design, including air operated doors and a full front streamlined body. With such heavy bus replacements in hand, it was clear that there would not be a great deal left for the new Marton trams. On the other hand, the track bill comprised not only the complete renewal of the Marton route, but also the relaying of track on the Promenade and Lytham Road. Work had begun in January on relaying the track over Skew Bridge, and also plans were made for diverting traffic from Lytham Road when the Promenade to Hopton Road depot approach was relaid. This was fairly routine compared with the publicity which accompanied the proposal to re-site the Metropole track. Mr Luff drew attention to his plans of 1937 for the re-siting, and the Town Clerk was instructed to obtain Parliamentary powers for running to the west of the hotel. Nothing had been done by December in that year, by which time the Surveyor reported that the old foundations of the track were breaking up and "the rails were moving on the curve". This alarming state of affairs resulted in the track being relaid as a matter of urgency in the same position, as it is today. Historically, it seems that the Metropole Hotel opposed this, together with the position of the War Memorial.

Meanwhile, all was not well with 208, and further work apparently needed to be done on the Crompton Parkinson Vambac equipment to make it more thoroughly reliable. Consequently, on 3rd February 1947, Brush car 303 was given the resilient wheel bogies again, while 208 had the other M & T experimental set with worm gears. Two days later, 303 was put into service on the Marton route where it must have looked quite strange amongst the tall Standards of a different generation. The residents of Marton were thus given a sample of the sort of trams they would enjoy once the track was relaid. At this stage, 303 was still driven conventionally by Allen West controllers, and thus did not have the performance of 208. However, another disadvantage of 303 was apparently the air operated sliding doors, which slowed it whilst loading at the street stops. Number 208 was refitted with these bogies in May, when its bogies were swopped again with 303. However, various trial runs were made in July and August, including testing on the sharp curve in front of the General Post Office in Abingdon Street. It was essential to determine the success of the new equipment before further sets were ordered for the Marton cars. Meanwhile, during August the track renewal continued along Whitegate Drive as far as Marton Depot, leaving a gap until Vicarage Lane where it resumed along Waterloo Road. The gap here was deliberately left since the Ministry of Transport were planning a traffic island in Oxford Square. The rate of progress with the relaying was such that it was confidently estimated that the work would be complete by October. One of my friends who went to Waterloo Road School recalls watching the track men Thermit welding a rail joint outside his school one dinnertime. It was quite fascinating, first they heated the rails till red hot and then set fire to the manganese in its crucible. With dramatic suddenness it fell with waves of heat above, and so the rails were fused together. To his dismay my friend found that watching this interesting scene made him late for afternoon school, and his curiosity was rewarded by some dramatic strokes of the cane!

At Easter 1949, addressing the Light Railway Transport League, Mr Luff claimed that there would be trams in Blackpool as long as anyone present might be living. "Trams in Blackpool were reliable and still operated at pre-war fares of a penny a mile, while the Transport Department contributed one thousand pounds a month to the rates". When consideration of the Marton route was under way, people told their councillors that they had wanted their trams to continue. This optimistic note continued throughout the year, with interesting developments on all fronts.

Mineral traffic at Thornton Gate sidings finished on 1st May, and the sight of the little green electric loco pulling a train of clanking coal laden wagons was gone for ever. Tram drivers were glad to see the back of

Views of welding track in North Albert Street, Fleetwood in February 1990, showing first fitting the crucible over the clamped rail-joint, and then the burning magnesium filling the rail-joint. This is how the rail-joints were welded on the Marton route in 1949. *(Author)*

the coal wagons for the last time, having been made late many times while following them slowly, and waiting for their shunt on to Thornton Gate sidings. Another reminder of the past vanished in 1949, when the remaining track from the Layton route between Talbot Square and North Station was tarred over on 17th June. This had been used for Standards going from Talbot Square to North Station, to provide relief for heavy crowds on Dickson Road, especially on Saturdays during the Season. This enabled the former Layton tram terminus to be removed and an island terminus for the Marton route provided, completely segregated from all other traffic. There was still one more section of the Marton route to complete between Marton Depot and Oxford Square, and after the advice of Walter Luff for safety, it was relaid during June and July. Thus by September the Borough Surveyor was able to report that the whole route had been relaid and that he was discharging most of the track-gang employed to do the job.

The customary extension of the Marton service to South Pier at Whitsuntide, entailed the addition of two further sun saloons 13 and 14 to the route. While Marton Depot now had five, it had the unusual addition of open-top Southampton 45 which arrived from Leeds to be stored for the LRTL. Passengers who saw its arrival might have been wondering whether they were witnessing a ghost from Marton route's past. However, it did not appear again, until it was presented to the new Tramway Museum Society in June 1955, and today runs at Crich Tramway Village. Meanwhile at Rigby Road depot, a pair of the first production Maley & Taunton HS-44 bogies arrived on 27th June. Sun saloon 21 had been prepared for its new role during April and May, and alteration had also been made to the underframe in order to mount the 6ft wheelbase of the new bogies. However, there were some faults to the brake framing and rubber suspension, and they were

(Top) Devonshire Square stop in 1949 with the track-relaying finishing, and Standard 48 contrasting with the approaching sun saloon bound for Royal Oak. *(RR Clarke)*

(Right) Talbot Square terminus with Standard 158 and the first Marton Vambac, number 21, admired by a group of tram enthusiasts. *(FEJ Ward)*

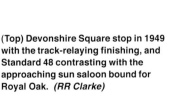

15

sent back to the manufacturer. In October alterations were made to receive the Vambac equipment for mounting in No. 21, including a panel in the roof of the platform and hinged ventilating louvres on the four sides of the trolley tower. This would enable inspection of the rotary accelerator. The Vambac equipment was fitted in November and by 2nd December the car had been painted ready for service and became the first to be called a 'Marton Vambac'.

It happened that 1949 was also the first year of the post-war Illuminations and the Publicity Committee was anxious to have a new illuminated tram for that occasion. When asked, Mr Luff offered the alternative of decorating the open Boat cars in bunting and fitting all cars operating on the Promenade with fluorescent lighting. In response, the Publicity Committee tried again and this time Mr Luff said that it would only cost £500 to rewire the Lifeboat and Gondola so that they could appear in the Illuminations. A new illuminated tram fitted with a motor generator and fluorescent lamps would cost £2,500, and so the Committee told Mr Luff to provide a modern illuminated tram by autumn! To meet their demand, the pre-war Bandwagon, which had been used during the war depicting slogans, still existed and the body-builders got to work on giving it a new appearance. In 1937 it was built as an illuminated tram on the frame of old Fleetwood crossbench car 141, now it was made taller and took the form of a double-decker with 'shadow' passengers in the windows and holiday slogans along the sides. At the front it carried 'PROGRESS' – by which it became known, and in the centre of the sides was a giant Tower, and the whole car was a blaze of lights. When the Illuminations appeared on 16th September for the first time in ten years, the Progress car, along with the Lifeboat and Gondola, were the centre of attraction. All Blackpool people turned out that night – including myself – and it was one of the most memorable in the town's history. As a child I was thrilled when the glowing Progress car arrived and it played music as it passed, while I heard many people wondering whether you could ride on it!

Elsewhere 208 was being used on the Promenade, a number of drivers having been given instruction in the new technique. One driver was heard to say: "That tram is so quiet that the holidaymakers on the Prom can't hear you coming!" However, 208 had proved itself, and some interesting figures compared its performance with that of a bus, speed taken at five second intervals: Bus: 11.3, 18.3, 25, 29 mph in 23 seconds. Tram 208: 16, 24, 30.5 mph in 17 seconds. The speed of 37 mph was reached in each case.

It can thus be seen that the Vambac system allowed the tram a much greater rate of acceleration in the first ten seconds until 24 mph, after which there was levelling out. The maximum speed of 208 was modest compared with its potential of four 45hp motors, but with this equipment would consume 4.5 units per car mile which was greater than the other Blackpool trams. Therefore, it is understood that the field-shunt equipment was eliminated, to avoid the faster running speed of over 40 mph, as seen on similarly equipped cars in Europe. With this satisfactory experience to draw upon, it was decided to order 18 sets of Vambac equipment and 18 sets of HS-44 bogies, enough to equip a complete Marton service of 15 cars with three

Progress car seen in 1953, decorated for the Queen's Coronation and expressing the wish 'LONG MAY SHE REIGN'. *(The Gazette)*

A pair of Marton Vambac cars in Talbot Square, this class now having taken over the route. The livery with flares only lasted for a few years. Notice the lights on the towers, for the Illuminations. *(John Fozard)*

spares. On 12th December 1947, Walter Luff submitted the two quotations which he had received, and these were accepted. The Maley & Taunton HS-44 bogies were to cost £2,748 per pair, while the Crompton Parkinson Vambac equipment would cost £2,300 per set, thus costing £5,048 for each tram.

The 1939 sun saloons 10-21 were selected for this reconditioning, along with six 1937 Brush cars, which would resemble them in appearance. In December 1947, work began on making sun saloon 10 as a more acceptable car for the Marton route, and the work was carried out in Blundell Street depot, including fitting a centre roof with fluorescent lighting, soft-cushioned seats replacing hardwood ones and new signal bells. The exterior was painted in the new livery like 208 and 303, with green flares on cream panels. On 18th January 1948 it became the first modern service car on the Marton route, and was followed in April and September by 11 and 12. At this time they were conventional cars with their original equipment, but they compared favourably with the Standards, giving the passengers a sample of what new cars they could expect in the near future. No more cars were altered at this time, since it was felt that it would be better to await the arrival of the new bogies and equipment, so that the whole conversion could be completed at one time. On the Promenade, the other nine sun saloons were still in use, giving the passengers a hard ride on the wooden seats. I always remember getting on such a tram in Fleetwood and being surprised, having never seen a tram with a glass roof and wooden seats before!

A view from balcony Standard 40 following a service car up Clifton Street passing the Tivoli Cinema and heading towards the impressive GPO building in Abingdon Street. *(John Fozard)*

A delightful view of Church Street with the Vambac car waiting at the traffic lights outside the Regent Cinema, and Blackpool Grammar School building seen behind. *(John Fozard)*

In many ways 1948 marked an interlude in the refurbishment of the Marton route, with most of the track relaid and new equipment on order for the trams. Apart from the three sun saloons in service, the Standards continued in their traditional way. However, the school children from the numerous schools served by the route did not like the new single-deck cars, because on the Standards they could ride on the top deck enjoying themselves, out of the view of the conductor. Meanwhile, in Fleetwood it was reported that boys had been riding on the rear fenders of trams between Ash Street and Broadwater, thus finding single-deck cars useful! Marton route was not long out of the news, however, for Mr Luff was pressing to have the Clifton Street track relaid in the same position. Although in 1938, it was proposed that the line should follow the old Layton route up Talbot Road turning into Abingdon Street on the outward journey and returning down Clifton Street. Also on the Borough Surveyor's track-relaying list was the Dickson Road route, which was twenty-five years old and due for renewal. It was also planned to relay the Bispham Depot track-fan, and a tender was received from Edgar Allen for £3,500 to provide this pointwork. Interesting to note that manufacturers supplying rail to Blackpool at this time included Hadfields of Sheffield, the Skinningrove Iron & Steel Company of Salthouse and Dorman Long of Middlesbrough. Bull-head rail for the sleeper-track was priced at £17-8s-0d per ton, while groove-rail cost £19-15s-11d per ton, being controlled by the Iron & Steel Control Council. Special work was renewed on South Promenade during the year, and the loop at Fleetwood Ferry was renewed. Thus, it was clear that the future of tramway operation in the town was assured for many years.

Before the end of 1949, another important step for the future was taken since Mr Luff had been reporting upon the need for new tramcars, pointing out that a deputation might visit Stockholm and Copenhagen to see new types of trams in service there. It is true that PCCs had appeared as trial cars, but they did not last as did those in The Hague and Brussels. His desire for new cars to be single-deckers met with opposition by Councillors who felt that double-deckers would have been better for Blackpool. However, Mr Luff was convinced that the single-deck cars – like the American PCCs – were the trams of the future, and he contended that passengers preferred to ride on them, that they were easier to clean and maintain and lighter on the permanent-way. In the event he succeeded and by November in that year quotations were invited for 25 single-deck tramcars 8ft wide and 50ft long, with resilient wheels and automatic control equipment. It was clear this latter factor was influenced by the success of 208 with PCC-type equipment, and this seemed to be the only logical development. By March 1950 the Transport Committee had received ten tenders for the 25 new trams, and the Light Railway Transport League commented: "this effectively disposes of the myth that new trams are unobtainable in Britain." In retrospect it is worth considering that the new cars may have been intended to replace the double-deckers, which were significantly still in the wartime livery at this time.

Meanwhile, the steady conversion of the sun saloons to Marton Vambacs proceeded during 1950, and since their English Electric bogies of 1939 were surplus, a new role was sought for them to play. At first it

18

was thought that the Standards would be worthy recipients of these bogies, and in November 1949 Standard car 39 was lifted and its Preston bogies exchanged for those from 16. Since the car was not air equipped, the air brake fittings were removed from the bogies. After a trial run on 10th December, 39 was ready for service and returned to Marton depot. All did not go well for 39, after two days the brakes were locking on the rear trailing wheels, and since this was not a success it was decided to use this pair of bogies under a 1928 Pantograph car fitted with air brakes.

In April 1950, Pantograph 173 became the prototype for changing its bogies, receiving those from Marton sun saloon 11, and joined the North Station and Fleetwood service on 4th July. This change was a success, for the Pantograph cars had air brakes and therefore 173 did not have the difficulties which were experienced on Standard 39. Accordingly, cars 175, 174 and 171 were soon converted, making good use of the 1939 bogies, but 39 continued to be a liability on Marton and was withdrawn. In the normal routine, Pantograph 176 was brought from Bispham Depot in October for a change of bogies, but this proved to be a one-way journey. At this time thought was being given to passenger flow on a tram, and 176 was used for a trial in Blundell Street depot to have a front entrance made on the near-side only. After inspecting 176, Mr Luff decided to cancel the idea and 176 was left in that depot, with no new bogies and becoming the depot shunter of withdrawn trams. Unfortunately, it joined the withdrawn Standards there and was duly scrapped with them by 1954. Also in Blundell Street depot at that time were five of the 1927 toastracks 162-6 and the illuminated trams. In contrast, on the other side of the depot the conversion of sun saloons to Marton Vambacs was taking place. Here all the bogie changes were effected to these and eight of the Pantographs – not 167 and 174 – together with body modifications to the sun saloons. The early delay which had been experienced in waiting for the new Vambac equipment had left 20 raised on jacks in Blundell Street depot early in 1950. However, once delivery started, it was not long before there were over 40 sets of Maley & Taunton HS-44 bogies lined up in the depot. Twenty-five of these sets were for the new cars, the bodies of which were being constructed by Charles Roberts of Horbury in West Yorkshire. Thus the second Marton Vambac 20 entered service in June, cars 19 and 18 following in August and December respectively. Simultaneous with the re-equipping of 16-21 was the body modification, and thus on Marton services there were Vambac cars and six sun saloons at the same time. At this time Leeds Transport continued to show an interest in the Blackpool experimental cars, and in June its Manager Mr Findlay and Chairman Councillor Rafferty came to see if

Vambac 15 in Abingdon Street on the last day of the Marton route, 28th October 1962. (Peter Fitton)

Pantograph 174, now fitted with modern EE bogies, whose driver
is manually switching the points for the North Station route,
having missed the skate in the overhead. *(John Fozard)*

they could borrow a tram for trial in their own city. However it seems that their size was against such a transfer, thus depriving us of a unique scene of 208 or 303 in City Square! Meanwhile, drivers reported defects with the trial cars, although 303 had different experimental bogies while 208 had been fitted with new Vambac equipment in elegant gantry casing. It was expected that these would go to the Marton route but 303 never did, again reflecting the problems of its sliding doors.

Appropriately, it was in its 50th year of 1951 that the Marton route had predominantly modern trams, with the introduction of a further nine Vambac cars to the service: 21, 20, 19, 18, 17, 16, and then 10, 12, 14 in that order. The Marton summer service, extended to South Pier in June, required 15 cars running on a three-minute headway, and so the Standards had to be used as a supplement. It was rather an adventure for me at that time, waiting at a tram stop on Whitegate Drive after a day in Stanley Park, and wondering whether the next car would be tall, green and traditional or long, cream and modern. For the anniversary of the

A morning view outside Marton Depot, as 225 leaves for the Promenade, and so
passes the service car for Royal Oak. *(John Fozard)*

At Spen Corner the service car is followed by a Ribble Royal Tiger saloon, on service X60
from Manchester. Seen from balcony Standard 40 returning to depot. *(John Fozard)*

route, special green notices were printed and pasted on all the Marton cars and in all the shelters on the route. Each notice read:

**TRAMS WERE FIRST RUN ON THE MARTON ROUTE ON 1st MAY 1901, SO THAT ON
MONDAY 1st MAY 1951 THEY WILL HAVE BEEN RUNNING FOR FIFTY YEARS**

To celebrate the event, Marton depot was decked overall in flags and bunting, and undoubtedly part of the rejoicing was that the route had survived and now had the best tramcars in the town! A three-minute service meant that you never needed to run for a car, because the next would not be far behind. The comfortable interiors of the Vambac cars and the brightness of their fluorescent lights defeated the notion that trams were outdated. By March 1952, Marton Vambac cars 11 and 13 had joined the fleet and 208 followed soon after, making a total of thirteen modern cars. Of course there should have been a further six Vambac Railcoaches, but they were transferred with conventional equipment to replace the Standards. By May the first Coronation car was delivered, and was the centre of attention, leaving the Marton route to operate successfully. In retrospect, Blackpool had shown leadership, but nationally trams were being withdrawn, including London. However, the Marton route lasted for ten years, until it was closed in 1962 with its modern Vambac cars as the final British street tramway route. The cars were excellent performers, comfortable in which to travel, but with their centre entrances they needed a crew of two, unlike the PCCs which always had a front entrance and centre exits and carried more passengers. Thus, by 1962 the reduction in passengers, increase in road traffic and costs of operation inevitably saw the demise of the route and its trams.

Royal Oak junction with two Marton Vambac cars passing on the South Pier service,
with the Tower seen between them along Lytham Road. *(John Fozard)*

The crowd at North Pier watch the first Coronation making its inaugural run on 16th June 1952, with the Mayor at the controls and supervised by Walter Luff. *(The Gazette)*

The Coronation Trams

The finance of the Coronations was an important factor in the quotations of 1950: the bodies were quoted at £4,902 each and therefore a total of £122,550 by Charles Roberts & Co. of Horbury, the Vambac equipment was £2,503 per set by Crompton Parkinson of Chelmsford costing £62,575 for 25 trams, and the bogies at £5,765 per set by Maley & Taunton of Wednesbury was £144,125 in total cost. Therefore, the full cost of the 25 new trams was £329,250, or £13,170 each Coronation. When the first of the class arrived on 2nd June 1952, delivered by Pickfords at noon, it was clearly the largest tram dimensionally, and certainly the heaviest single-decker at 21 tons. Mounted on its bogies 304 went out on test on 7th June, followed by the Board of Trade inspection on the 11th. Walter Luff showed the Transport Committee a plaque to be placed on 304 to commemorate that the bogie and electrical equipment had been on exhibition at the Festival of Britain 1951. Its first public debut on the Promenade took place on 16th June, when a huge crowd assembled at North Pier to watch the Mayor of Blackpool in formal morning-dress drive 304 over the crossover, before its journey to the Pleasure Beach. One of the passengers was comedian Jimmy Edwards, who was allowed a try the controls by Walter Luff. The first trip to Fleetwood followed on the Sunday, with myself – at the age of 11 – never to be forgotten, standing in my bedroom window and seeing the sight of this impressive large tram for the first time.

Number 304 entered service on the Fleetwood route on 3rd July, and more followed during the year, until 310 appeared in December. However, there were queries by the Transport Committee as to whether the new trams could travel on the other routes, especially the relaid Marton route. Accordingly, it was arranged on Wednesday 6th August at 23.00 for 305 to give a demonstration from Talbot Square to Marton depot. Walter Luff timed this deliberately to avoid parked cars standing next to the right-angled curve into Abingdon Street, where the overhang of 305's body could have hit such vehicles. The press pictures provide the impressive sight of a Coronation in the town centre. It is understood that this journey was sufficient to provide the evidence, not risking its journey over the bridge at South Station to Royal Oak. Of course, it was Walter Luff's intention that the Coronations would be operated purely on the Starr Gate and Fleetwood service, which was the busiest and most famous location for the trams. Acknowledging their smart appearance the new trams were known as 'Spivs' by the staff; drivers found them fast-running, and the first four cars had field-shunt equipment allowing them to accelerate even faster. One driver coming off his turn said: "I've been catching seagulls with that tram!", when he finished his duty. Unfortunately, this drained the current-feeder system from sub-stations with mercury-arc rectifiers, and I remember Sundays when trams were static in Fleetwood and probably elsewhere. Also another of the early problems with the Coronations was the whip action of the long trolleys fitted with large swivel heads, which dewired and

Coronation 305 in Abingdon Street on its first and final trial journey to Marton. *(The Gazette)*

had to be shortened and fitted with fixed heads. Also I remember seeing Coronations being towed back to depot, usually by a Pantograph car, providing an ironic contrast!

In 1952 Walter Luff reached the age of 65 and would normally have retired, but the Transport Committee asked him to continue for another twelve months, during the delivery of the Coronation cars. The first day in complete service by ten of the Coronation cars – 304, 305, 306, 307, 309, 310, 311, 312, 313 and 314 – was on Tuesday 10th March 1953 – a market day. Apart from that significance, on the same day Marton depot supplied 23 trams – including eleven Vambacs on the route – and others on the Promenade, plus nine football-specials using Lytham Road and not the original pre-war Central Drive. Also in 1953 there were two significant dates to record, since on Saturday 2nd May Blackpool Football Club won the FA cup at Wembley Stadium, beating Bolton Wanderers 4-3, on this memorable occasion. On 2nd June it was Coronation Day and all the trams were confined to depot in the morning, when television took command for the first time. Appropriately in 1953 the Coronation cars were fitted with commemorative plaques showing E II R in the centre of the trolley towers. Then on July 7th the Fylde Coast was visited by aircraft carrier HMS Eagle, and free tram rides were given to the visiting officers and sailors of the ship. Many local people went by boat for a cruise round the HMS Eagle, but it proved choppy for the author! Another date of significance in the history of Blackpool Tramway was the 26th July when 112 trams were in service during the afternoon; comparing this with the maximum of 40 trams in 2005, times have indeed changed. In the Illuminations that

year, on 5th September, the Gondola went out for a TV test and BBC Television car 166 made a trial run along the Promenade two days later. On 9th September the TV car left the Pleasure Beach at 22.10 followed by the Gondola and Lifeboat for filming, and the latter was occupied by the famous Lancashire comedian George Formby. Beginning with New Year's Day in 1954, the three depots had an output of 62 trams being in public service: 34 from Rigby Road, 14 from Marton and 14 from Bispham. In contrast these days, there are no trams at all running on New Year's Day.

Toastracks 166 and 165 on BBC Television Service at the Tower in September 1953, ready for televising the Illuminations. Notice the cameras and floodlight on the roof. *(Maurice Marshall)*

Coronation 304 in immaculate condition, ready for its inaugural run to Fleetwood for the Transport Committee. Today this part of the depot is the electrical compound. *(Author's Collection)*

(Below) Coronation 308 at Little Bispham for Starr Gate on route 23 in the late 'fifties. *(John Fozard)*

(Facing page upper) A delightful scene at Fleetwood Ferry with two contrasting Coronations, 316 on the left having been repainted without chrome beading on the front, fixed standee windows and now with an enclosed panelled roof. *(Dennis Gill)*

Walter Luff made his last annual report to the Transport Committee in June 1954, in which he said: "So much money has been taken out of the undertaking for rate relief, that new vehicles have to be bought out of reserve funds." Hence the Coronations were bought with borrowed money, and the huge total of £500,000 was repaid by 1968. Successor JC Franklin became General Manager on 15th July, having been the Manager of Rochdale and Chief Engineer of Salford, fulfilling his aim to run Blackpool Transport. He subsequently recalled: "Prior to taking over, I only had one meeting with Walter Luff, and I asked him about the finance of the one hundred new buses from Burlingham, and also said "I believe that you are having a lot of trouble with the new trams", and he replied "Well we've had a bit of trouble, but nothing serious." While visiting the Works, the Superintendent said: "Mr Luff, I've got fourteen Coronations off the road", upon which we moved out of there like lightning! Mr Franklin continued: "My first weeks were an eye-opener, and I found that the Coronations certainly had problems. Basically the bodies were too heavy for the bogies, hence the component failure of the bearings and broken axles. He then called in representatives of Maley & Taunton and Charles Roberts Company to see what could be done. Under threat of legal action, new bearings were made by Maley & Taunton, and Roberts gave £1,000 towards body repairs. Maley & Taunton then fitted eight new bearings free-of-charge, which cost £112 for each car and, therefore, £2,800 for the 25 Coronations. The faulty bearings and the rubber sandwiches in the wheels put great stress on the axles, and thus they broke regularly and so a new set was made in Blackpool. Mr Franklin remembered that on several occasions wheels actually came off, though fortunately it happened when the cars were stopping or starting. To compensate for the weight, the cars were re-panelled in aluminium, replacing the steel panels with which they were made originally. This started with 316 in 1955, and at the same time the chrome beading was removed, which had been the source of rusting to the panels. Also, he recalled on one occasion seeing one of the opening standee windows fall out, and consequently they were replaced with fixed glass panels. At an early stage – which I can remember – the roof windows leaked and were first remounted, and then panelled over to make a wider roof.

Ironically, the Marton Vambacs had roof windows without this problem, and thus remained until the withdrawal of those trams in 1962. Mr Franklin stated that all this situation with the Coronations indicated their "costly failure", and he always felt that the Transport Department was wrongly burdened with so much debt at a time of falling revenue. Quite apart from the problems that the Coronations created, undoubtedly the passengers – including myself – liked them, since the trams were more spacious than the pre-war Railcoaches, gave smooth riding with comfortable seats and gave good views through their many windows. I know as a seasonal conductor that the drivers experienced failure of the electric brakes, including the track brakes which should be used for emergency stopping. Consequently, it was necessary for the electricians at the depot to blow clean the rotary Vambac on a daily basis, and thus ensure that dust or sand did not prevent making contacts, essential for accelerating and braking. The maintenance of the 25 Coronations in the depot thus took most of their time, and the conventional trams at Rigby Road depot were somewhat neglected because of this.

To summarise, the verdict on the Coronations would suggest a mistake for the design of the body including the centre entrance based upon the previous Railcoaches. It seems that the future of the Coronations in Blackpool would have been more secure if they had been built in the PCC style, with front entrances and centre exits. Thus, they could have been eventually manned with one driver collecting fares, as in the replacing OMOs. At 20 tons for 56 seated passengers they were also excessively heavy. In due course, the cost of spare parts for the Spivs was becoming astronomic – especially the rubber sandwiches – because of the smaller quantities ordered. Re-equipping twelve of the Coronations with EE controllers was designed to keep them running, starting with 323 in 1964. Once the loan was repaid in 1968, Joe Franklin decided to phase them out, starting with scrapping disused 313, which was mounted on EE bogies at the back of the depot.

A familiar breakdown scene in Fleetwood, outside the Engine Sheds, with 309 and 318 heading a long-delayed service, owing to the blown sub-station breaker at Copse Road. (Author)

(Left) An interesting scene at Cleveleys in 1953, as a Balloon turns for 'Squires Gate and Airport' on Sunday morning, while a Brush car on service 1 waits for it to cross over. *(John Fozard)*

(Centre) Balloons of the second series – with rails in the front upper windows and hoods over the windscreens – are seen passing at the Cliffs. The wooden laburnum tree indicates that it is autumn! *(John Fozard)*

(Below) A 1960 busy line-up outside The Savoy, headed by the pioneer Twin-car set 276 and 275, followed by Panotograph 171, a Boat and Brush car. The trolley has passed over the skate which operates the points for North Station, and the skate after the frog on the Dickson Road line would reset the points for the Promenade when passed over. *(John Fozard)*

(Facing page) Inaugural scene on Central Promenade, with 277 towing T1 after presentation of the first trailer by manufacturer Metropolitan Cammell-Weymann to the Mayor of Blackpool on July 25th 1960. *(The Gazette)*

Apart from this focus on the Coronations, certainly for JC Franklin the priority for improvement was to the double-deck Balloons. About them he said: "I was astonished to find that the double-deckers had never run to Fleetwood, and on enquiring to the Ministry of Transport, I was told that check-rails would be needed to stop them overturning. So we bolted on miles of angle-iron to the track, which would not have stopped a tram from turning over, but satisfied the Transport Ministry!" On 1st July 1958 the first Balloon on No. 1 service from North Station to Fleetwood helped to take crowds to the Market and bring them back. Undoubtedly, their large seating capacity made them ideal to assist the overcrowded single-deckers, in contrast with Walter Luff's original policy, double-deckers made an unusual sight, after the tradition of the Blackpool & Fleetwood Tramroad.

Further fleet developments took place on 9th April 1958, when the Progress Twin-cars 276 and 275 made the inaugural journey to Fleetwood for the Transport Committee and the Mayors of the Boroughs. Prior to the 1957 rebuilding of the two Railcoaches in the Works, visits were made to Zurich to assess the operation of trams with trailers. It was clear that the planned Twin-cars would carry 114 passengers and thus were regarded as having useful increased capacity to move crowds, with the provision that trailers could be disconnected and parked on sidings at off-peak periods. A decision was made to purchase ten new trailers, made by MCW of Birmingham and bogies by Maley & Taunton. The first trailer, numbered T1, arrived on 16th July 1960, and was first towed by 277 for presentation by MCW on an inaugural run on the following Tuesday. Others were delivered at intervals during 1960, with T9 and T 10 arriving in January 1961, completing the delivery. The appearance of the trailers in all-cream livery was similar to the style of the Coronations, and the towing-cars were rebuilt in the same style. However, they were first used on Coastal Tours, which proved to be less successful than the Boats on Promenade Circulars, since the distance of 22 miles was too long. Thereafter, the Twin-cars were used as specials, being able to reverse only at Little Bispham or Fleetwood northbound and Pleasure Beach and Starr Gate southbound. Consequently, beginning with 281-T1 in November 1962 followed by a further six Twin-sets, they were permanently linked as two-directional units to make them more flexible. Three of the towing-cars 278-80 could be operated individually, which resulted in three trailers T8-T10 being disused and subsequently scrapped in 1981/2. Fortunately, the Twin-cars began operating service duties on the Fleetwood route in 2003, when track relaying precluded the use of the Balloons. This was the first time they became service cars after 40 years, and they continued during 2005 along with the Balloons. In retrospect, it seems that acquiring articulated cars from Europe would have been more useful to Blackpool than the Twin-cars. However, in the 21st Century, new articulated cars may yet appear on the route between Starr Gate and Fleetwood.

A fascinating scene in the Body Shop with Dreadnought 59 newly fitted with folding steps and upper-deck panels, joined by ex-conduit car 4 still fitted with the snowplough in February 1960. *(Author)*

The 75th Anniversary

The Promenade Tramway's 75th Anniversary fell in 1960, and Joe Franklin was determined to stage a remarkable procession on 29th September. It was indeed fortunate that four historical cars had survived, three of them as Engineering Cars whilst Dreadnought 59 had been saved by Walter Luff in 1935, after a public appeal by the Evening Gazette. "Sometime in the future it may be possible to resurrect the old Dreadnought car and parade it on the Promenade as an example of what people in Blackpool used to enjoy travelling on." The Dreadnoughts had been withdrawn in 1934 after the delivery of the new open-top double-deckers, and so 59 stood in Copse Road depot all those years, without its trolley mast, wooden seats and wide end-steps. During the winter of 1959, one night it was towed back to the Body Shop by a Railcoach, where it was restored to its traditional appearance.

There was however, an even older survivor. At the back of Bispham Depot, I always remember seeing a tiny open-top car in faded dark green livery, but with a trolley mast and vestibules for the driver. It was replaced as a works car by 31 in 1934, but was retained because it had been conduit car 4 of 1885. It was pleasing to hear that it was driven from Bispham Depot to the works, still being in working condition. A great deal of work to restore its original appearance meant removal of the platform vestibules and side saloon doors when used as a works car. However, it was renumbered 1 and painted in the red and white livery used by the Borough from 1892, and labelled "THIS IS IT !" over the driver's platform.

Two of the Blackpool & Fleetwood Tramroad Company cars also still existed in the form of Crossbench car 2 of 1898, numbered 127 and based at Copse Road for engineering work, whilst Saloon 40 of 1914 was based in Rigby Road depot and transported the track gang to and from Copse Road depot each day. It was numbered 5, in green livery, and had windows painted cream. The four vintage cars were ready for use in June 1960, but No. 1 was restricted for tours and special processions. The Tramway Museum Society had a tour on 9th July, with 1, 2 and 59, and while 2 and 59 went to Fleetwood, car 1 had to stay at Bispham until their return. However, this was a sensation, being the first time that a Dreadnought had been seen in Fleetwood. Consequently 2, 40 and 59 were used on Promenade Circulars from the Tower each day, and were very popular with the public. On 29th September a procession in each half of the day was held from Pleasure Beach to Little Bispham, giving free rides to the public. The procession posed on the Little Bispham loop for the press and BBC television, but the passengers had to stay on board. Certainly the procession effectively showed the development of the fleet over 75 years: 1885 conduit 1, 1898 Crossbench 2, 1902 Dreadnought 59, 1914 Box car 40, 1924 Standard 40, 1928 Pantograph 170, 1934 Railcoach 217, Boat 236 and Balloon 249, 1953 Coronation 321 and Twin-car 276-T3 of 1960. This was a triumph for Joe Franklin, in order to illustrate the historical importance of the Promenade Tramway after 75 years. Retired Walter Luff declined his invitation to come, perhaps because he liked to be associated with modernising the fleet!

The scene at Pleasure Beach on 29th September 1960 as the 75th Anniversary Procession is loading with passengers, headed by ex-conduit car 4 – now wrongly numbered 1 – but THIS IS IT! *(WGS Hyde)*

A contrasting scene at the Tower seen from Balcony 40, as Crossbench car 2 waits for passengers on the Promenade Circular, and the Railcoach passes on the Squires Gate and Bispham route. *(John A Senior)*

Other Trams Blackpool Could Have Acquired

Throughout Britain, the replacing of trams by buses in post-war years, resulted in the transfer of trams to other systems. First, Blackpool was offered the two English Electric streamlined double-deckers by Darwen, but they were too small with 4-foot gauge, and in 1946 Llandudno & Colwyn Bay Electric Railway took them. Then Manchester Pilcher cars were sold to four systems: 14 to Aberdeen, 11 to Edinburgh, 6 to Sunderland and 7 to Leeds. The largest class of trams transferring from London to Leeds were 90 Felthams in 1950/1, which with larger capacity went into service on the cross-city routes of York Road to Whingate and New Inn. Later they were on the circular Middleton route, climbing though the woods on a private right of way and returning via the new Belle Isle route. Of course, this preceded the decision in 1953 for the trams to be replaced by buses by 1960, but certainly gave us the opportunity to sample London Feltham cars, albeit on a different system. The final example has to be the acquisition of 46 Liverpool Green Goddesses by Glasgow in 1954-6 in order to add to the Coronation and Cunarder modern fleet of 252 cars. Although it had been decided to prune that system using a nucleus of 300 modern-type trams, it was not until 1957 that complete replacement of the trams was decided. However, suitable trams elsewhere could have joined Blackpool's streamlined fleet of the 'thirties.

By this time in the 'fifties, Rochdale General Manager JC Franklin, was pleased to become Manager of Blackpool Transport in 1954, but found he had inherited the debt from purchasing 25 Coronations which became something of a liability, as already recorded. However, during the 'fifties, Blackpool was successfully operating the four-route tramway with a fleet of 157 trams, and clearly may have been interested in good second-hand streamliners. An approach was made by Aberdeen which had 22 double-deck streamliners, of which two were originally built by English Electric in 1940 and 20 in 1949, under licence by RY Pickering of Wishaw. The relevance to Blackpool was that under the 'Five Year Plan' fifteen smaller double-deckers were to be built for the Marton route. Plans were drawn up by the English Electric Company, for a tram which was a shorter version of the 1934 Balloons with a three window saloon and 72 seats. Once the Second World War started in 1939, it was impossible to start the relaying of the Marton route, and buy new streamliners to replace the Standards. Undoubtedly, the Aberdeen streamliners would have looked appropriate in the fleet, especially since they had a green and cream livery with flares, and seated 72 passengers. Like Blackpool's, the Aberdeen streamliners originally had two conductors, but in 1952 the situation changed when they were fitted with air centre doors operated by the driver, whose vision was improved by having wing mirrors and longitudinal seating in the lower saloons. I know that JC Franklin did go to Aberdeen to see them, but he declined the offer on the grounds that they were "narrow gutted and slow", being 7ft 3ins in width, and, unfortunately, they were all scrapped. In retrospect, I feel that they would have been suitable for the Marton route, but subsequently that route closed and the Aberdeen cars could have proved useful on the Promenade and cheaper than the Balloons. However, this is wishful thinking though and it may appeal to your imagination!

The other interesting offer of trams in 1959 concerned the three single-deck streamliners in Leeds, which seemed to be appropriate for Blackpool. Number 600 was a rebuilt Sunderland car while 601 and 602 were

Roe-built, the latter being all-electric with Crompton Parkinson Vambac equipment and Maley & Taunton bogies. Joe Franklin visited Leeds and was taken for a ride on 602 along the York Road reservation. When I asked for his opinion, he said "I have examined the Leeds single-deck tramcars, and they were much too small for our operation and therefore unsuitable for our type of work". However, the original intention was that such cars could operate with trailers and run in a subway though the centre of Leeds. Although this never materialised because of converting the tram system to buses, ironically 50 years later Leeds has tried to revive a modern tram system across the City. The Blackpool Manager's decision may have been right, but Leeds City clearly made a mistake in closing a well-planned tramway system in 1959. However, today we can still ride on Leeds 602, albeit at what is now called the Crich Tramway Village in Derbyshire.

It remains to mention the other post-war trams which might have been suitable for Blackpool, starting with the Sheffield Roberts cars. Being 4-wheelers they were not ideal for the sleeper track on Blackpool's reservation, and this was subsequently proved with the derailing of 513 in 2003. Finally, the Glasgow Cunarders were undoubtedly handsome in appearance, built by Coplawhill Works and equipped with the Maley & Taunton bogies, four Metro-Vick motors and electro-pneumatic control equipment. By 1962, when the Glasgow system closed, Blackpool was in the same situation, since it was closing the street routes and consequently the fleet was to be reduced in size. Of course, we never thought that we would see a Glasgow Cunarder on Blackpool Promenade, but No. 1297 came from the National Tramway Museum in 1984 ready for the Centenary. Undoubtedly, it performed well on the sleeper track, and subsequently returned to Glasgow for the Garden Festival in 1988. To summarise, Blackpool tramway has been a survivor in the age of tramway closures in Britain, and has utilised its fleet – largely 'thirties streamliners – in order to operate effectively. In reality, Blackpool has only acquired other trams on loan for historic occasions.

With the closing of tram routes throughout Britain, it seemed inevitable that the Blackpool routes would follow. In 1959 there was an attempt to close the North Station route, but the General Manager made a very precise report upon the value of the line. In 1960, soon after the 75th Anniversary, it was announced that the Squires Gate route would close in 1961, due to the worn track. The last tram was 268 but without ceremony. However, on 28th October 1962 a closing ceremony of the Marton route was held at the depot, since it had become the last street tram-route in Britain. On 27th October 1963, the North Station route was closed, leaving only the Promenade and Fleetwood route remaining. The depots at Marton and Bispham were also closed, thus centralising the fleet of buses and trams at Rigby Road.

(Facing page) Aberdeen streamliner 37 shown on the Hazlehead reservation and heading for Sea Beach with a familiar English Electric-designed body. *(Dennis Gill)*

(Below) In August 1959 two open days were held in Swinegate depot before the closure of the Leeds system, and seen here are Vambac 602 and Feltham 526 with railcar 601 behind – a unique scene! *(Author)*

End of the Marton Tram Route

(Above) A final day scene outside Marton Depot on 28th October 1962, showing 13 and 17 in service and 48 on the third track loading for the tour by Blackpool & Fylde Tramway Historical Association.

(Below) Standard 48 as the last tram at Royal Oak before finally leaving for Marton Depot and showing its wreath and tributes, together with a group posing in front of the tram . (Peter Fitton, both)

(Facing page above) On the last weekend of the North Station route, 26-27th October 1963, there was a final tour on Boat 225, seen here in Red Bank Road on returning to Bispham depot loaded with enthusiasts. (John Fozard)

(Centre) A delightful scene of 147 at North Station, with Talbot Hotel and a group of enthusiasts capturing it – including the author! (John Fozard)

(Below) Number 290, the last tram from North Station and Fleetwood, enters Bispham Depot watched by the enthusiasts who have put their coins on the track to retain a souvenir. (Author)

My Final Year Of Conducting The Coronations – In 1964

The author standing in front of 318 at Fleetwood Ferry – with the indicator set to Squires Gate, which was not possible for trams at this time.

You may have previously read my accounts of being a point-boy and tram conductor for Blackpool Transport from 1959-63, but for the first time here is an account of my experiences of working on Coronations from Rigby Road depot. With the closure of the street routes to Squires Gate and Marton in 1961/2, and finally with the closure of the North Station and Fleetwood route in 1963, Bispham Depot closed and the staff either trained as bus drivers or drove trams on the remaining coastal route. Consequently, in 1964 as my final year, I was based at Rigby Road for the first time, although I had worked from there on 'specials', including Standard 159 and Crossbench car 2 in 1962. However, until then, I had never guarded a Coronation, and so I hope my reminiscences of that experience will be interesting.

Back on the platform

We came out of the depot on my first morning on Coronation 321 into bright sunshine. While reaching for the trolley with a pole, I caught the frog-wire and received the wrath of the depot fitters and electricians, who maintain such fixtures. My response was that they needed to provide a longer trolley-pole! So we set off down Hopton Road, 321 rattling and rumbling over the Manchester Square junction. On this early turn we first did Central Station to Starr Gate, which necessitated getting my hands dirty because of being the first conductor to handle the trolley-pole. The first journey down South Promenade is always a rather nice one, because the driver can try his car's paces. Thus 321 was travelling along at speed with that roaring noise and periodic sounding kok-kok from the wheels, on the occasional rail-joints between welded sections of the track. There were no passengers at this time of day, which gave me a first chance to write these impressions as a tram conductor in 1964.

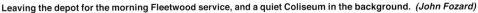

Leaving the depot for the morning Fleetwood service, and a quiet Coliseum in the background. *(John Fozard)*

A business run on 325

We left Fleetwood on Coronation 325 at 8.07am for Starr Gate. It was the sort of trip I liked, busy with passengers at each stop and enough time to collect one lot of fares before the next stop. All was very efficient, me quickly using the TIM ticket machine and bracing myself against the next rheostatic braking which can throw you off balance. On 325, my driver Harold found that the air brakes were weak and thus he had to use the electric rheostatic brakes right up to the stop, with the result that there is a sudden jerk with a refined howl from the motors. You have to brace yourself against the terrific deceleration, which could cause you to fall. When we left Cleveleys at 8.27am, we had a full seated load, and just as we topped the gradient from Anchorsholme, I saw Railcoach 270 move from the loop and swing on to the main line in front of us, bound for CENTRAL STATION. This route 102 covered the main service on a busy trip at peak hour, we then picked up the odd passenger for further destinations. I noticed that 270 was full when it climbed out of Gynn Square, and without its help we would be leaving passengers behind. This is the sort of tram operation that one likes to see: efficient, busy, good time-keeping and regular passengers with the right change for their fares! This is so much better than the holiday-makers who don't have the change and are not sure of their destinations. There is nothing to beat regular passengers of shop and office workers who know their fares to their destinations. At Manchester Square 270 turned into Lytham Road and momentarily recreated the Squires Gate service car, until I saw the replacing service 12 bus. The shining strips of rail down Lytham Road disappeared under the tarmac, while the lines swing into Hopton Road for the depot. It is now after 9.00am and the visitors are emerging from their hotels to make a busy day.

Wind and sand affects Coronations too

These two elements in combination are the common feature of the Blackpool scene, and one which has effects on the trams. Gale-force winds blow sand into every nook and cranny, windows become grained and difficult to see through, while the cream livery becomes stained and sand-coloured. Working on the trams in these conditions, you eat sand in your sandwiches and you feel grit under your feet on the platform. When the doors are opened, the air reservoir blows it up from the ground into your eyes. Apart from the personal disadvantages in these conditions, they present technical problems of their own. Yesterday my driver Harold said that he had trouble in getting away from Manchester Square in a Coronation, because the sand under the wheels prevented earth return. He said there were fireworks coming from the Vambac equipment. Another driver was telling me that he was coming out of Lytham Road on a Balloon and he had to stop for the traffic policeman, but when he was waved on he felt a bit of a fool when the car would not move. This was because there were huge patches of sand across the rail. One of the Inspectors came to the rescue with a trolley-pole, the hook of which he used to make contact between the wheel and bare rail. Thus in a series of fits and starts the car was able to move forward in jerks. It is true that sand stopped the conduit system in 1885, and still affects operation whilst using the overhead system today.

Manchester Square, with Coronation 314 about to pass Standard 159 followed by the Western Train. *(Author)*

Coronation 309 in North Albert Street squeezing past a parked Rover whilst approaching the 1902 Post Office. On the other side of the road Parkinson's Grocers Bradford Jowett van is parked at the tram stop. *(John Fozard)*

An evening at Fleetwood in July

A good Spiv is really a king among trams, tonight we are on 312 – a very nice car! The pleasant evening emphasised the smoothness of the ride, the bogies most recently having been overhauled because there is no rattle, just a delicate tap-tap, tap-tap on the rail-joints. There is a faint whine of the motors – just an octave above the normal. The compressors, when running, make a quiet pattering sound too, and together they indicate the ideal. We stop in Lord Street at the Preston Street stop and looking from the platform at the reflection of 312, I see the long cream shape with a green band round the middle. Once the passengers have stepped off and are walking to the pavement, I ring the bell. There is a hiss from the air brake, a rising whine as the driver pushes the control stick forward and there is a rattle from the Vambac rotary converter above the platform. We are zooming forward with acceleration, and as we pass along the street I see 312's moving reflection in the changing shop windows, including myself standing in the open doorway. The wheels sound kok-kok, kok-kok as the bogies go over the crossover in North Albert Street, and we are soon turning sharply into Bold Street and ideally arriving early at the Ferry, for a welcome cup of tea.

Learning to drive 314

Working as a conductor, we were at Fleetwood Ferry 10.19pm and without any passengers. Driver Harold went 'round the corner', and so I went to sit in the cab with the saloon door shut. Seated there, it seemed a strange situation because it does not resemble a traditional tram. With all the gadgets around, I feel that it resembles a spaceship! With my right hand I pushed the forward/reserve key into forward, and eased off the air brake from right to left which made the hissing sound. With my left hand I pushed the accelerator stick forward, and as I did there was a rattling sound from the Vambac rotary converter above the centre platform. The car glided smoothly forward with an increasing whine from the motors, and 314 turned the curve into Pharos Street. When I pulled the stick back, little happened and I had to put the air brake on to halt the car, and easing it off and on to avoid a jerking stop. The Spiv is such a big car that it was quite a thrill to be its driver, even for a short distance! Harold, returning from his visit, said; "Well you've done well, are you going to take over for the rest of the journey?"

In the busy peak season

We are now in the busiest weeks of the year, and Blackpool is packed with pleasure seeking crowds. Working on the tramway there is a wide variety of interest for the observer. In addition to the Spivs and Brush cars on the Fleetwood route, Balloons have entered service today on routes 1 to 10. The Santa Fe train on Circular Tour provides a startling reminder of the autumn days of the Lights ahead. It always attracts your attention since it is prominently colourful in contrast with the green and cream trams. Today, looking from a 25A bus in Dickson Road, I saw it in profile climbing up the Cliffs from Gynn Square, and it looked quite striking with its smokestack and cab. Standards 158-60 are a welcome feature of the scene, representing traditional types of trams in contrast to the streamliners. This lovely evening is especially good to describe, when our tram was rocking and rolling down the hill from Bispham, the sun was reflected on the sea and the shipyards at Barrow could be seen along with the cluster of mountains in the Lake District. The coast curving to Rossall Point could be seen clearly, and the trams provide ideal mobile observation platforms! The men who first built this line for the Blackpool & Fleetwood Tramroad Company in 1898 certainly had terrific foresight. At that time the Tramroad would be more dramatic running through the open fields on the cliffs, while it is now urban with lines of houses and hotels. The attractiveness of this line, especially along the cliffs, turns one's thoughts to the future – how long can it last when trams have disappeared throughout the country? (Fortunately it has lasted another 43 years so far!)

My journey to work today showed that the buses can be quicker, when there is less traffic on the roads. Trams can be unpopular with visitors at the Pleasure Beach, where they wait in a line with their doors shut, except the first one loaded. Surely it would be good initiative to load several cars at the same time? This cannot detract from those occasions like last Tuesday when load after load of people were taken to Fleetwood

A delightful view of Coronation 321 in Lord Street, as seen from the clock tower of the Co-op building in 1966, with an interesting variety of cars and buildings, including the Regent Cinema in the background. The full roof of the tram is shown, with very clean paintwork. *(Author)*

Newly painted Coronation 316 while still a Vambac car in 1965, turning into Pharos Street and leaving a Twin-car at the Ferry. Not everyone liked the orange trolley tower. *(Author)*

Market in full Balloons. Thus trams can move the crowds – a slogan for their use! Also the Standards are useful and indicate sentimentality with their green dash and twisting staircases, recalling their street operation in the past. It is a fitting epitaph today, that after 80 years there is no case against the value of the Blackpool trams! (Still true today in 2007.)

Turning at Ash Street by night

I have poled a car many times at Ash Street, but never at night. On our last trip on 322 we were at Cleveleys when we should have been at Fleetwood, so the Inspector told us to transfer our passengers to the car behind and display ASH STREET on the indicators. As we left Cleveleys, I ran through the indicator and found little-used destinations like NORBRECK and ROSSALL and finally found ASH STREET. We let the next service car round us at Thornton Gate, and thus we were empty when we got to Ash Street. I divested myself of the cash bag and the ticket machine in preparation for my athletics ahead. As we ran over the points, I jumped off and seized the point-bar which I rammed down the nearest point-blade and checked the other one just in case! Two patrolling policemen viewed the proceedings with disapproval from the other side of the road, but this is not a crime! I swung the point-iron over its hook, pulled the trolley-pole down from its pole-rings and hooked the trolley-boom securely. I was holding the pole at head height to give maximum pull-down. There I stood in front of the tram, waiting for Harold to run through the saloon with the 'knife and fork' and the time-card. Entering the cab, he rammed the forward and reverse key into the slot on the right of the controller-box and put the air brake handle in, releasing it with a deep sigh from the air reservoir. Suddenly the car moved forward, the lights of 322 dimming down as it traversed the crossover. I stepped backwards to one side and started running round with the trolley. As I pulled the trolley down the lights went out and there was a violent hiss as the platform doors slid shut. The momentum of the car and the length of the trolley swung me towards the kerb. I reached the back of the tram, while it was still moving across and I looked up to see the shining copper wires. I deftly thrust the trolley-wheel upon the far left wire, which hit it with a smack. The lights came on and the doors opened, so that 322 came to life and the job was done. I replaced the pole and jumped back on to the platform refitting the TIM and cash bag, a few passengers boarded at Ash Street. We were then in service and returning to Starr Gate again.

A disadvantage of working on 310

When Harold met me in the TIM room, and told me that we had got Spiv 310 today, I groaned. This is one of the experimental Spivs on the road, and is the worst from the guard's point of view, because it has 64 bus seats which face forward in the front saloon and backward in the rear saloon. The result is that passengers are always changing ends, as soon as the front salooon seats become vacant. Another feature which is a mistake, are free sliding doors without controls. The fitted weak spring grips mean that on acceleration and

Above: A view from 59 at Cleveleys Square in 1963, showing the Spiv reversing for STARR GATE, while the Inspector holds back the Brush car on the North Station service. *(Author)*

deceleration the heavy metal doors slide open or shut with a thunderous crash, thus startling the passengers. This will result in many platform accidents! Another fault of 310 are the bogies which rattle in a deplorable way, making the riding thoroughly noisy. The only redeeming feature which I can find, is that the gangways in each saloon are wider and it is easier for a guard to collect fares. However, it is less comfortable for the passengers sitting on smaller seats.

On the way to Fleetwood at 8.31am we went through the middle line at Bispham to pass a Balloon bound for Cleveleys. As we went through the sprung-points, the car shook. I leaned out and watched the trolley-head, and when we cleared the bottom points with a clatter, I saw the frog coming up. As I watched, the wheel rolled off and flew up in the air. Remembering the same last year with Spiv 328, I did not try and ring the bell instead shouted loudly to the driver, and he stopped 310. Since there were some trolley-poles at the side of the track, I managed to hook the trolley-boom about 4ft from the end. As the tension is greater at this point, I had to pull the trolley hard. It was rewired at the first try, and driver Harold said: "it's a good job – since you're tall". At Fleetwood he told me although I had shouted to him, he could tell it was dewired because the lights in the cab went off, and so he put the air brakes on immediately.

Number 270 becomes an unlucky Railcoach

We seem to be unfortunate having 270 today, since the last time we had it, a boy dropped a tin of paint on the platform during the teatime rush-hour! On our first trip we were late and therefore had to turn at Harrowside, but we had become so late that the Inspector at Broadwater told us to turn at Ash Street.

(Left)   The bright spacious saloon of a Coronation with fling-over seats, seen at the Fleetwood terminus.
(Right)   The saloon of 310 with the 64 bus seats facing in opposite directions on each side of the aisle.

A maritime view of 270 at the Ferry with the dredger sailing in, and the lifeboat house behind the tram. *(Author)*

There was great consternation amongst the passengers who had booked to the Ferry, but a Spiv was following behind to take them. At each stop I had to shout "Ash Street only". Then to my surprise lads with three kestrels got on at Lindel Road. At Ash Street, as the passengers left us, I divested myself of the cash bag and TIM, and prepared for a quick turn-around. I dropped off as the tram passed Scotch Bakery and rumbled over the points, and grabbed the point-iron from the hook on the pole, moved the points over and dashed back for the trolley-pole, and hooked the leading trolley as the tram was driven towards me. I pulled the trolley down and let it swing round as the tram moved passed me, and I was pulled behind the tram and I aimed the trolley-wheel on the wire. When I tried to lift the hook off the trolley-boom, it stuck to the binding tape and jerked up, so that the trolley-wheel ran over it and dewired. The following Spiv hooted, showing the amusement of the driver! On our next trip we had another piece of bad luck. As we approached Rossall Beach, I noticed the farmer from College Farm turning off Broadway in his maroon car, but he continued in front of the tram and 270 hit the motor car's rear wing. Immediately, there were exchanges of addresses and witnesses between the drivers. When we arrived at Talbot Square we found that the lights would not work and reported it. With no regrets we turned 270 at Pleasure Beach for returning to Central Station, where 289 was waiting for the change-over, and we left 270 again.

A typically busy Saturday morning in August

As this is one of the last Saturday mornings I shall probably work as a tram guard, I think it is worthwhile to record those special features on a tram in Blackpool. This morning having drawn my TIM, I walked past the line of Leyland Orion buses towards the depot, where Spiv 323 stood on the curve into track 18. I glanced at it and hoped we had not got it today, since it proved to be a dead loss in service. I shouted to Charlie – the good-natured depot shunter – and asked him where our tram was. I could not recall the route number on the time-card which is always shown in the driver's cab, but I knew that we were to be out at 7.09am I told Charlie and he said: "Oh, your tram will be over on track 17 then". On track 17 there were three Spivs, the first of which was 326 which would be ours. I got on and wrote all the times of the journeys on my waybill card for the day, while driver Harold ran backwards and forwards trying to get the doors right, but they remained obstinately shut. So Charlie had to come and sort out the door switches so that we were then ready to go. Harold, sitting in the cab, released the air brakes and so with a whine and a lurch 326 started moving forward over the pit. The door reservoir hissed as we passed under the dead section of the depot door runners. Once outside, there was a noise from the wheels as 326 took the curve – that distinctive deep and yet hollow sound of the Maley & Taunton bogies - and yet there was the sound of clattering as the wheels crossed the worn point work. We passed Charlie hanging on to the frog-wire and he told us to take the car right down to Hopton Road to turn the trolley. Then we set off for Central Station and reversed 326 for Starr Gate. We were 8.31am from Fleetwood, and on that journey we started carrying the returning holidaymakers and their cases mounted on the centre platform. This would be a busy day, carrying the departing and arriving holidaymakers, and the platform would be loaded with piles of luggage – ideal on a spacious Coronation.

Trams and their passengers in 1964

Visitors are an unadaptable race at Blackpool, where they are faced with a situation which differs slightly from the norm – Britain's last remaining tramway. I suppose even in the 'thirties, the Blackpool centre entrance trams were a bit different; now 30 years later when these are the only trams, they have unique problems. My most frequent cry as a conductor is "Both sides on please", facing the passengers with a fatal choice, which way to go? Inevitably, they all follow the leader through the doorway, and then half of the family goes one way and half goes the other! Passenger flow with a front entrance and centre exit would solve the problem, but 120 centre entrance trams raise the obstacle. A Coronation is best for loading quickly, with its large double doorway and wide gangways, enabling people to get on and off with ease. The opposite of this must be the Standards with large platform steps to defy the old ladies, and the angular and winding staircases which test the strength of mums and dads, while the youngsters bound up them to be 'on the top'. The fact has to be that people are softer than they were 30 years ago, when skirts were longer and more voluminous. Of course, the present generations are more experienced on buses than the 40 year old trams. Another thing which the public are inexperienced in are the reversible seats, which they persist in turning contrary to the direction of travel, so infringing the regulations. Perhaps the most annoying habit from a guard's point of view is the habit of asking "Two to Central" without giving the right numbers of their family.

Passengers come in many types, those who are wearing hats with the names of the pop-group, and those who jump on to the tram and immediately ask "Six 5d – that's 2/6". "Well done", I answer. "I don't trust conductors", said the passenger, as I issue the tickets correctly. In the 'sixties tight skirts and stilettos presented problems boarding the trams. The stilettos got stuck in the groove of the sliding-doors, suggesting that modern fashion is not always compatible with tram riding. Also, police officers were seen free-riding and, therefore, standing on the platform. However, it is interesting to contrast the visiting passengers with the Fleetwood residents for whom the trams are the norm, as they swarm on without instructions and usually have the correct fares ready. They habitually curse the vistors who fill the trams in the season, which leave them standing at Ash Street after a hard day's work.

The thing about being a tram guard is the variety which it presents, thus the car is made ready at the depot in the morning, turning the indicators and the seats, while the dewirement of any tram stimulates a challenge to show dexterity with a bamboo pole. Being tall I usually fare well, as with Spiv 319 which de-wired yesterday. We staff are comrades on this tramway today, which is perhaps because we are staffing a unique form of transport.

Single-line working at Foxhall in 1959 requires the trolley of 318 swinging on to the northbound overhead. Notice the remains of snow, with the shovel leaning against the duty-man's hut – the sun doesn't always shine in Blackpool! *(RP Fergusson)*

An unfortunate scene in 1964, as a Coronation is being pushed back to the depot by a Brush car, and catching the attention of the changeover crew at Manchester Square. The policeman has probably seen it all before. *(Author)*

The case of Brush cars *versus* Coronations

Nicknamed 'Mods and Rockers' (who were a feature of the 1960s), today I have guarded Brush car 294 for the first half and found it shocking. We have mainly had Spivs – or 'Mods' – for the last few weeks, but 294 was constantly a 'Rocker'. For a start, in contrast with the spacious Spiv, a Railcoach seems cramped and you have to push past knees, dogs and children to get along the narrow gangways and collect the fares. When passengers are boarding there is not enough room for a conductor to stand by the bell. As soon as there are eight standing passengers, it means having to hold the TIM ticketmachine in your hand, taking a deep breath and squeezing past people which is not very pleasant on a wet day. It seems strange when I have worked Brush cars from Bispham Depot, although they were more suitable for the quieter North Station route. In addition, these cars now have the manual sliding doors opening and shutting themselves, and rattling sounds from the perspex light covers. In contrast, how different is a Spiv, with that commodious 6ft platform and those two 3ft doorways with the centre pillar fitted with the bell and the door switch so the conductor can stand centrally, with passengers boarding at each side. Occasionally, it is possible to channel the passengers getting off through one doorway and boarding through the other. In the saloons there is room to move more freely, getting past each other in the gangway. With the drunken crowd which has just got on at the Cabin, I must add that a major advantage is that the space of a Spiv enables you to keep a distance. The Vambac equipment has other advantages; for example, the initial surge of power enables you to get away from stops quickly, consequently avoiding unwanted fighters, drunkards and runners. As the control switch is turned, the hiss of the doors encourages passengers to hasten on and find their seats. In contrast to the jerk of the series notches of a conventional controller, the glide of the Vambac equipment ensures that a Spiv has smooth acceleration. These are the chief contrasts between the 'Mods and Rockers' tramcars. For this guard, whatever the driver or engineer can say, the problems of centre entrances are minimised by the size of the Spivs as an advantage. (Subsequent to 1964 Spivs were withdrawn and scrapped, leaving the small Brush cars in service until the present day. Thus, engineers can claim to be right!)

My last service tram– 11th August 1964

On this night we are the final Fleetwood tram from Talbot Square at 11.45pm and, as we waited at Cabin, I reminisced about previously doing this duty from Bispham Depot. My driver – while on a night tram – said that he once chased a cow along the track at Rossall – hopefully matters will be quieter tonight. Time to move off and we worked down to North Pier, reversed on to the centre track and put a blank on the indicators, until the final THORNTON GATE tram went in front of us. We then put FLEETWOOD up, took the

This could be 40 years ago when I described working on the Coronations. However, it shows 304 and 324 in Bold Street Fleetwold on 8th November 2003, on their first tour together. *(Author)*

passengers, clocked 11.56pm at Bispham and 12.05am at Cleveleys. At Fleetwood Ferry it was all quiet and I clocked my time-card with the 'ting' echoing in the stillness. Along Lord Street the ribbons of steel shine in the street lights ahead and the walls of the buildings echo the roaring of the tram's wheels as we make our lonely way along the thoroughfares, so busy during the day. The inky blackness across Rossall fields was eerie, with the invisible track guiding our way as we bounced and swayed like a ship on the ocean. At Cleveleys, in the strange silence, we wait for our time of 12.43am together with the flashing of the Belisha beacons for the empty pedestrian crossings. A single headlamp swings into view and works car 3 passes us with the familiar whine of the motors accompanied by the unfamiliar roar of the diesel engine which is driving them. As it clatters over the points, it picks up speed and vanishes into the silence of the night. Our final journey rolls on, with the empty saloon glowing as a beacon of civilization and I complete my waybill with readings from the TIM before we return to the depot and I finally pay in the cash. I hope that reading my notes written at the time will give you some insight to working on the trams – especially Coronations – in 1964! Steve Palmer – conductor 3604.

The depot in 1964 with cream Coronations, together with Balloons advertising Empire Pools of Blackpool, and just as I remember it. *(Author)*

Railcoach 211 on the traverser, having been winched out of the old Body shop,
just visible inside, the Coronation car is being repanelled – January 1962.
(Author)

Behind The Scenes
– A Major Reorganisation

The Central Repair Works dates originally from 1920, when it was built on the old Highways Yard in Rigby Road with railway connections. As built it was somewhat like a tramway avenue with an approach line from Blundell Street to the traverser pit, and then the trams were carried sideways to the different workshops of Body Building, Lift and Fitting Shop, Paint Shop. The buildings along the traverser pit were former aircraft hangars which were joined together in order to create workshops which succeeded in producing 48 Standard trams by 1929, and maintaining them thereafter. However, changes in the 'sixties saw rebuilding of the site, and locations of the workshops as it is today. It is interesting to note that in the 21st Century some changes may take place again to change the layout of the Works to provide easier entrance and exit in parallel to Blundell Street. However, it will be interesting to hear how changes took place 40 years ago in order to function as it does today.

The first statement of a policy of centralisation was an announcement by the Transport Chairman in January 1961 that: "We are going to make more use of the Rigby Road centre and thus eventually dispose of the depots at Marton and Bispham". Clearly, this was linked to the closure of the three street tramways between 1961-3, which would involve total operation from Rigby Road and the increase in the size of the bus fleet. Until 1960 the Transport Department had been divided into 'Tramways' and 'Omnibuses', and was now to be merged under one Chief Engineer, Mr Eric Kay. It was his task to integrate tramcar and omnibus maintenance facilities. At first sight this might have seemed impossible, due to the different maintenance procedures of electric traction and diesel engines, but common body and painting facilities were needed. Until 1961 the tramway situation had remained static for post-war years, with three running depots at Marton, Bispham and Rigby Road and the Permanent Way depot at Copse Road in Fleetwood. Blundell Street depot, which had been replaced with the new depot in Hopton Road in 1935, had remained a store for surplus trams and their scrapping until 1956, when it was converted to a bus garage and its pits filled in. The central workshops for maintenance of trams and buses were situated between Blundell Street and the then main railway line to Central Station. The buildings were grouped in two sections each side of the traverser line, those nearest to the Coliseum Bus Station being the most substantial brick buildings housing the bus bodyshop, and separate bus and tram paintshops. The buildings housing the electrical maintenance, bogie overhauls and body repairs were in a line of corrugated former aircraft hangars, to the east of the traverser. Since there were many doors with tramway lines emerging to the traverser pit, buses crossing them to the garage gave a somewhat uncomfortable ride for the crew. In addition, the old aircraft hangars did not provide adequate protection from the weather on some occasions, and when the roof of the Body shop was damaged and had to be battened down in November 1960, it was decided that it was time that something was done. It was recognised that the approach to the Works traverser on a line next to the Transport Office proved somewhat time-consuming, and what was more important was that the traverser was space consuming. It seemed that it was necessary to merge the painting and body facilities, reinforced

A scene from the original Fitting Shop, in which can be seen two Railcoaches 281 and 272, being rebuilt as towing cars for the new trailers in May 1960. A Brush car can just be seen on the body lift on the right. *(Author)*

(Below) Balloon 254 (717) now on the body lift in the depot, seen in October 1964 with its bogies having been moved to the Fitting Shop. *(Author)*

when each had its labelled step ladders such as 'Tram Body Shop' and 'Bus Body Shop'. Each had its foreman and craftsmen, who had the same skills. Thus, it was decided that these workshops would be merged in the brick building to eliminate such duplication which was wasteful.

During 1961, the plans were drawn up with a concentration in the substantial brick building between the tram depot and the Transport Office, with the consequent demolition of the old aircraft hangars. The conversion of the Squires Gate tram route at the end of October resulted in an increase in the bus fleet, which gave urgency to this spatial problem. Buses were already being stored between the bus garage and the tram works. To allow the demolition of a section of the building as soon as possible, work was begun in spring 1962 on the conversion of the former bus Body Shop next to Blundell Street into the new tramway Fitting shop for overhaul of bogies. Work proceeded throughout the summer, for with the impending closure of Marton Depot at the end of October, it was evident that Blundell Street Depot would return to use for trams once again, thus displacing the buses which had been garaged there since 1956. The new workshop

Pantograph 170 with the rail carriers in front of Copse Road depot in 1962. The two stone plaques showing the Company and 'JUBILEE 1897' are still visible today. *(RP Fergusson)*

was completed by the beginning of 1963, and its floor space enlarged in such a way that all the machinery from the old Works could be re-positioned in a rational way. The first section of the old hangars, which contained the Lift Shop, was closed and demolished in January 1963, and the section of the traverser pit serving this building was filled in. The tram body lift was moved to the back of pit 11 in the depot, and it was thus possible to continue machine bogie work in the Works during this transitional period. This made more parking space for buses, and a corrugated wall was temporarily made for the remainder of the old Works.

At this stage, the closure of the Permanent Way depot at Copse Road in Fleetwood further indicated the pruning of the tramway buildings. During the last weeks of 1962, Pantograph Works car 170 and the electric locomotive were busy shuttling backwards and forwards between Copse Road depot and Thornton Gate sidings. They were engaged in moving the existing stock of grooved and bull-head rail, sleepers, chairs and pointwork to this new storage site, where the crane from Copse Road had also been installed. All the mobile items such as arc-lights, tie-bars, bolts and tools, were taken to a new Permanent Way store at Bispham Depot, where 170 and the locomotive were based when the move was complete. Following this, in 1965, 170 became illuminated Frigate 736, Bispham Depot closed at the end of the year and the locomotive went to Crich National Tramway Museum in January 1966 where it became a useful tram shunter. For a short time

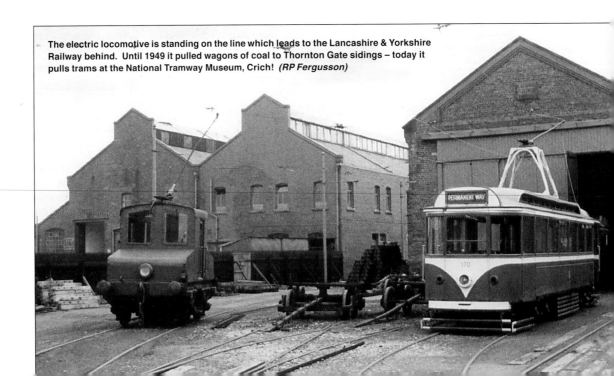

The electric locomotive is standing on the line which leads to the Lancashire & Yorkshire Railway behind. Until 1949 it pulled wagons of coal to Thornton Gate sidings – today it pulls trams at the National Tramway Museum, Crich! *(RP Fergusson)*

An interesting scene in the old Body Shop in 1960, showing Vambac Railcoach 208 with Dreadnought 59 and Crossbench 2 both being restored for the Anniversary in September. The structure of the building identifies it as originally having being an aircraft hangar. *(Author)*

Copse Road Depot remained empty until it was thought that the building might be purchased for a Transport Museum, and thus four historic trams scheduled for preservation were driven there and stored. From that day on 18th April 1963, when Crossbench car 2, Box saloon 40 and Standards 40 and 147 jolted over the grass grown points in the depot yard, the fortunes of the proposed museum fluctuated and finally failed. The first three of the cars were delivered to Crich in autumn, and 147 was stored in Blundell Street depot until it left for America in September 1967. Thus ended Copse Road Depot, which opened its doors to trams of the Blackpool & Fleetwood Tramroad Company in 1897. The building was sold and today is a car showroom, although the sub-station for the Fleetwood section is sited in the building. The stone plaques of the Tramroad Company and 1897 can fortunately still be seen.

Meanwhile at the Rigby Road campus, preparations were in progress for reopening buildings which had not contained trams for many years. The former municipal car store next to the Transport Office was fitted with new sliding doors and two tram tracks were laid in readiness for its new role as the combined bus and tram Paint Shop. At this time the tram traverser was still operating – albeit on a shortened track – to provide access to body and machine shops. In February 1963 the site of the Lift Shop was being concreted ready for buses from Blundell Street depot, which had to make way for the displaced trams from Marton Depot. Twenty-one trams filled the rear portion of Blundell Street Depot during the first week in March, and their presence made a welcome sight in this historic car shed. On Monday 11th March 1963 a small procession comprising Balloon 251, Gondola illuminated car 28 and Standard 48 left Marton depot for the last time, after which the power was switched off and the scrap merchants were left to complete their destruction of the trams there.

Under the Rigby Road reorganisation, the traverser was to be completely removed and replaced by a track fan which would give access to the new body and paint shops. This fan would be connected by a single line from the end of the depot approach, making a broad curve in front of the bus garage doors, and running along the site of the former traverser pit. Consequently, the shortening of the traverser pit was accompanied by the laying of the track bed for this new Works fan. Approach lines to the new combined Body Shop were laid in May, while the traverser still provided access to the old Body Shop. This transitional stage was completed in June, with the removal of the traverser – its controller was bought by Modern Electric Tramways for use at Eastbourne – and the connection of the two Paint Shop lines to the approach line. The new Fitting Shop was in full use by this time, enabling the old corrugated iron works section to be demolished. The last job in the old Body Shop had been the conversion of Railcoach 222 into the illuminated Shell Hovertram, and it was then transferred to the new Body Shop, making almost a complete circuit via the old traverser, Blundell Street, and the new Works fan. However, the old tram Body Shop was not without trams, since two Railcoaches 205 and 219 were isolated in the building and so were broken up there. It remained as a general store until finally being demolished, and a storage line across the former traverser pit was laid there.

Since the beginning of 1961, when the passenger fleet stood at 157 trams, there had been a piecemeal nibbling at the fleet total. The first two trams to be scrapped were Standard 41 and Marton Vambac 10, both accident victims which formerly would have been repaired. The closure of the Squires Gate and Marton routes resulted in the withdrawal of the majority of Pantographs cars, Marton Vambacs and first series EE Railcoaches. However, some had been scheduled for enthusiasts preservation schemes, and several other cars survived as illuminated cars: 168 as the Rocket, 209 and 174 as Santa Fe Train and 222 as the Hovertram. A group of 17 cars were broken up in Marton Depot in March 1963, five Railcoaches at Thornton Gate and seven more in Bispham Depot. The passenger fleet now totalled 122 trams. The compactness of the new Works is evident on the plans in comparison with the sprawling nature of the old Works, thus in keeping with the reduction in the size of the tram fleet. The corresponding increase in the bus fleet, as a result of tram route conversions, was achieved by the open bus park occupying the site of the old tram works. Because of restrictions to bus parking clear of the tram track and frequent bus movements there, poles for the overhead were not erected and therefore trams are towed to and from the new Body and Paint Shops to this day.

Behind the Scenes

In the two shops served by this fan, the concept of the integration of tram and bus body overhauls is very evident. The Paint Shop is a spacious building with two widely spaced tram tracks, which enables trams and buses to be painted simultaneously – in many colours today! In this way, the additional cost of separate tram and bus paint shops was eliminated. Next door is the Body Shop with two trams occupying the tracks nearest to the paint shop and up to four buses in the part of the Body Shop further away. Here all major repair and overhaul jobs to tram and bus bodies are undertaken, and in more recent times complete reconstruction of 633 as Trawler Cevic and 736 as Frigate HMS Blackpool have taken place. Machinery was moved from the old tram Body Shop and from the bus fitting shop to this new Body Shop, so that duplication was eliminated and bodybuilders worked in the same place. Today – 40 years later – the staff still deal with passenger vehicles in the same way. Adjacent to the Body Shop is the general stores, for easy access its entrance faces the bus park. From the Body Shop a doorway leads into the new Fitting Shop, where bogies are overhauled and varied machine jobs carried out as required. When seeing this Machine Shop one is immediately impressed by the orderly and logical layout of the building, which runs parallel to Blundell Street and the former Coliseum bus station, now Somerfield supermarket.

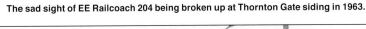

The sad sight of EE Railcoach 204 being broken up at Thornton Gate siding in 1963.

The new Fitting Shop in April 1964, showing Coronation 319 standing over the wheel drop pit. A pair of M & T bogies are nearby, and under the lifting frame a pair of EE bogies can be seen. *(Author)*

Trams requiring overhauls enter from the entrance opposite the tram depot. However, wider Coronation and Centenary cars have to enter from the north entrance. Two trams can stand over the inspection pits, and they are fitted with wheel drops in these positions. Running parallel to the main line and connected to it by a sharp crossover near the south entrance is a second track used only for bogies; this is flanked by a broad gauge track for the travelling crane. The forge is situated at the north end of the Fitting Shop, and the machinery and work benches are placed in two lines between the track and party wall with the Body Shop. The process involved in bogie overhauls will be described presently, and the reader will be able to get the best idea of the layout from the plan on page 59, and the various illustrations. All the machines are power unit driven, as opposed to belt driven line shaft machinery in the old Machine Shop. The workshops throughout are lit by fluorescent tubes which give the clearest possible working condition. Amongst the many jobs undertaken by the Fitting Shop have been the making of the pantographs and new underframes for the bodies of 72 year old trams, including the double-deck Balloons.

It will have been noticed that the three departments described above contain common elements which enabled integration between tram and bus overhauls to some extent. Of course, there are other servicing processes where 'never the twain shall meet', and it was the policy to provide specialist facilities in the tram depot and bus garage respectively. Thus, the electrical compound involved in rewiring trams has been located at the back of the depot and enclosed with partitions and doors, as also in the bus garage where the engine maintenance takes place. An increase in efficiency has been one of the aims of the centralisation policy, and this has been assisted by separating the maintenance workshops from the open depot and garage. Older readers may possibly recall the depot 'portcullis' doors which were raised and lowered by electric motors. These were a feature when this depot opened in 1935, but had the disadvantage of being susceptible to gale-force winds when they had to be opened. These were replaced by lightweight aluminium folding doors, which could be moved by one man and which concertina when open, thus taking up less space. Unfortunately, it was found that they could be caught by the overhang of entering trams and were removed, leaving the front of the depot open to this day. The second feature at the time of reorganisation was the 'Februat' tram washer, which by necessity had to be portable on rubber wheels. Being in two sections, when not in use it could be stored inside the depot. It was originally planned that it could be situated in Hopton Road, so that all cars could thus be cleaned as they came into the depot at night. Unfortunately, this idea was thwarted by nearby residents who complained of the noise and the fact that their windows were affected by the blowing spray. Subsequently, the washer was situated near to the depot where there are connections with the mains water supply. When a car returns at night, all windows have to be closed, and the driver applies one notch of power as the 16in nylon thongs drum on the panels of the car and the water covers it in a torrent of spray. For the crew a journey through this washer was quite an alarming experience! When a tram has thus been washed and enters the depot, it is boarded by a cleaner armed with a suction tube in order to remove used tickets and litter, which are sucked into a huge disposal drum. There are five vacuum

In August 1964, Standard 48 is being prepared for it to leave for Portland, USA, and the crews wait to take out other cars, possibly Balloon 247 (710) nearby. *(Author)*

lines, two operated by the bus garage plant and three by the depot plant. On each line in the tram shed, there are six or eight connections allowing for 50ft and 42ft trams in length, and corresponding with the position of tram doorways. A 30ft extension makes it possible for four trams to be reached and thus one vacuum line serves four pits. In this way the old job of emptying ticket boxes into a sack is eliminated. A common pool of cleaners suffices to undertake the longer job of thoroughly cleaning a tram by hand, which is now undertaken during the day. Today in the absence of the tram washer, cleaners use long brush hoses to thoroughly clean trams on a schedule but consequently they are not cleaned each day.

Let us now follow the progress of a tramcar through the workshops, and see just what is involved in keeping Blackpool trams serviceable, despite their age. Bogie overhauls do not necessarily correspond in timescale to the body overhaul and repaints, unless the car is to have full rebuilding. Mileages were originally logged by traffic staff and recorded for maintenance. However, today the bogies are inspected and setting for brakes checked by fitters in the depot, before the trams go out in service. Each month engineers from the Fitting shop inspect the tyres and brakes of the daily service cars. Re-tyring thus depends on the mileages in service; the Centenary cars presently are in use for 18 hours each day, and thus will do 35,000-40,000 miles before changing tyres every three years. In contrast, the double-deck trams are in use for half of the year, and their tyre changing takes place after 10-12 years. However, Jubilee 761 and 762 acting as substitutes for Centenary cars in service will cover 20,000-22,000 miles in the same period. Less frequently used, the Boats are re-tyred periodically, 605 taking place most recently. The procedure is that a tram will first be driven under its own power into the Fitting Shop and over the pit. Here it is completely disconnected, so that the body rests on the bogies without any electrical or mechanical connection between them, and then it is towed back to the depot and shunted on to pit eleven at the back of which is the lift. The body is raised to a height of about 3ft, which is sufficient to roll the bogies away from underneath. When the lift is raised in this way, a lower section between the rails enables a man to stand upright and therefore clean and paint the underside of the body. This job is completed while the bogies are being overhauled in the Fitting Shop. If necessary, it is possible to lift another car by using tram jacks on an adjacent pit. Next time you look into the depot you may see at least one tram towering above the rest in this way.

Once in the Works, the bogies are shunted over the sharp crossover on to the 'bogies only' track, and the first job is to remove the two motors. Should a defective motor happen to coincide with the overhaul, this motor will be taken by trolley across to the electrical compound in the depot. It may be necessary for it to be sent to a specialist firm for rewinding, as in the case of Box 40's motor in 2005. Normally the motor casing will be cleaned and given a protective coating of paint, while the armature is removed, the commutators recoated, and new bearings fitted if necessary. Before being refitted, the armature is tested on a special testbed just inside the entrance to ensure that there are no 'shorts'. Meanwhile, the motorless bogies are steam-cleaned by a mobile steam-cleaning unit. This job is usually done outside the entrance to the Works, and often clouds of steam swirl round the place making it like a Turkish bath! The bogies are then stripped down to the frame, and any part which is still dirty by reason of its inaccessibility is cleaned separately. The travelling crane running on the broad gauge track lifts the bogie frames and places them on stands, and thus there are no problems of moving such heavy pieces of machinery. The brake linkage is examined along

A winter depot scene in 1959 showing the portcullis down over most of the tracks – apart from those for the service cars like Coronation 304. Two young enthusiasts can be seen emerging from the depot. *(RP Fergusson)*

(Centre) The 'Februat' tram washer in action on OMO 12 as it is returning to the depot, showing: 'PAY AS YOU ENTER' *(John Fozard)*

(Lower) An interesting duty for Works car 4, as it tows a pair of EE bogies and a controller towards Blundell Street depot. *(Author)*

Coronation 317 in the Fitting Shop over the wheel drop pit, with EE bogie frames in the foreground, ready for cleaning and repainting in January 1964. *(Author)*

with all other moving-parts, and any welding which has to be done is undertaken in the appropriate location in the Fitting Shop. The two forges situated at the north end, with their attendant rows of blacksmith irons, perform essential functions in the repair of fractures and the manufacture of 'spares'. Compressors are examined and tested, new piston rings being fitted if required. Perhaps the most interesting part of the overhaul is that which concerns the wheels. Having been detached from the bogie frames, the wheels and axles stand waiting for attention. One by one they are lifted by crane to the 'gas ring' where the badly worn steel tyres have to be removed. The full wheel and axle is suspended by block and tackle, which lowers the wheel into a recess in the floor, where the tyre is surrounded by a tubular ring from which gas is brought to bear upon it. The 'gas ring' or 'gas tyre heating furnace' as it should be called, creates sufficient heat to expand the steel tyre, enabling the wheel to be raised from the ring, leaving the worn tyre behind. Before a new tyre can be fitted, the wheel must be allowed to cool. Because this takes hours, it is more usual to cut up the old tyre with oxyaccetelene equipment. New tyres as delivered by the manufacturer are fitted on the boring mill adjacent to the gas ring, the inner surface being machined until it is completely symmetrical.

Every type of tram will visit this place, including Rocket 732 seen in August 1977, with EE bogies in the foreground. *(Author)*

When this job is complete, the new tyre is ready for heating in the furnace, and finally the wheel is lowered into the expanded tyre. Upon cooling, the steel contracts and the tyre thus shrinks on to the wheel, gripping it tightly. When a pair of wheels has been retyred in this way, they are carried to the large wheel-and-axle lathe, which is situated next to the 'gas ring'. This impressive machine accepts a full wheel-and-axle assembly, and turns down the new tyres to the correct profile, so that the flange fits into the track-gauge. The wheel-hubs are 22ins in diameter and the full wheel with tyre is 27ins across, giving a tyre thickness of 2½ inches. It is interesting to note that Standard 147 has 30in diameter wheels, and in 2000 eight new tyres were obtained from Brussels for fitting. As each wheel and axle is completed, it is lifted by the mobile crane into a position adjacent to where newly cleaned and repainted bogie frames stand ready to receive all the overhauled machinery which goes together to complete a tramcar bogie. Piece-by-piece the bogie is reassembled, new cast-iron brake blocks being fitted in the process. Thus the overhaul process is complete and this set of bogies leaves the Fitting Shop in tip-top condition, although English Electric and EMB bogies are now 70 years old!

The routine overhaul just described has excluded reference to a special provision in the Fitting Shop for emergencies. In the event of a car having a broken axle, it can be driven over one of the two pits so that the wheels concerned stand upon a section of rail which is removable. The bogie frame is then jacked up so that the weight is taken off the pair of wheels, and the section of track unbolted allowing the axle and wheels to be lowered on a special rail trolley in the pit. The trolley carries the assembly transversely to the open recess at the side of the pit, where it is lifted out and carried to a position between the pits by a block-and-tackle. Here the rail trolley is brought into use for traversing the Fitting Shop to the metal press, which removes the wheels from the broken axle.

New axles as delivered from the manufacturer have to be machined to a degree of perfection which is extremely demanding. The removable section of track is known as the 'wheel-drop', of which there are six in three positions in the Works. It is also interesting to note that in the 'sixties one Coronation car was always lifted to provide a float pair of Maley & Taunton bogies. This became 313, which stood on heavy trestles at the back of pit 8 in the depot, and later in Bispham Depot until January 1966. The greater mileage which this type of bogie completed between overhaul can be attributed to the fact that braking shoes grip an external drum and not the steel tyres. These braking drums have to be turned down on the lathe during overhaul, and can be easily removed from the axle by unbolting. It should be noted that Maley & Taunton supplied tyres for their bogies ready-machined. The solo Coronation 660 in the fleet does little mileage now compared with its use as a service car, and preserved 304 was equipped with newly tyred bogies before its departure in July 1975.

Following the bogies being reunited with their tram again, all the equipment is reconnected, meaning that it is mobile once again. Now beginning the other half of a full overhaul, a tram is driven to the end of the depot fan, its trolley is tied down or pantograph lowered and it is towed over the works fan into the

A pair of English Electric 57 hp motors newly restored and waiting to be fitted to their bogies. Notice the four power leads hanging down, and the gears to engage the axle drive cog-wheel. *(Author)*

Profile of the Maley & Taunton bogie, showing the outside disc, to which the brakes are applied, the reversed leaf-spring supporting the body contact-discs at each side and the track-brake shoes between the wheels. *(Author)*

Body Shop. Depending on what has to be done, it will be there for several weeks. In the 'sixties, EE Railcoaches and Brush cars had their sliding sunshine roofs removed and the cars were refitted with a complete roof. Cross-members had to be inserted in the space created, and on to these tongue-and-groove boards were fitted. Over this went the traditional canvas roofing, given a thick coat of primer and the covering canvas coated with linseed oil. The canvas was then stretched across the painted boards, and the paint allowed to dry and harden, soaking into the canvas in the process. The front domes had to be reshaped to fit the new flush roof, although on many Brush cars a ridge was left between the old dome and the new roof. Following this process, some Railcoaches had new lower domes made and a flush metal aluminium roof fitted. Also streamlined cars of the 'thirties first lost their side indicators and then curved roof lights, the last such Brush car being 636 in 2003. Today aluminium panels are used on the roof, though fibreglass was fitted to the roof of restored Standard 147 and to to ensure that there are no 'shorts' 12ft teak panels along its sides. Traditionally, the side panels are examined and replaced where necessary by aluminium panels, and new window frames are fitted, as in the recent case of the Centenary cars and several Balloons. The last 40 years output of the present Body Shop included the building of the thirteen OMO cars and the Jubilee cars 761/2, together with rebuilt illuminated cars like Frigate 736 in 2004. Of course, routine repairs to damage in accidents and compensating for the wear to body-frames in 70 years make a clear role for the Body Shop. Their resourcefulness in the 21st Century follows the previous example of building over 40 new trams in the 'twenties, albeit in the original body shop.

Coronation 317 over the wheel-drop pit and a detached wheel in the foreground. *(Author)*

In January 1964, Railcoach 269, later OMO 1, having been repanelled in the Body Shop, is about to be shunted into the Paint Shop. This view shows the traverser and the old Works, now the Bus Park. *(Author)*

Trams which have been repaired and repanelled are shunted into the Paint Shop. Here they join other trams or buses which have come directly from the depot for a repaint. Firstly, the new panels are given a coat of primer, while the old panels are rubbed down and touched up with undercoat. Two coats of prime colours are then applied to the exterior with two coats of varnish to follow. All this is done by hand, and the finish of a newly painted car is superb. It is intended that a tram repaint should last for four years, although it has been the practice in the past to re-touch cars with varnish during this period. When this Paint Shop was new in winter 1963, no less than 19 Brush cars were painted in the new simple livery with cream panels, green upper saloon and an orange tower. Since that time in the 21st Century, liveries have changed from green and cream to a variety of different bus routes, also applied to different trams. Naturally, traditional trams are repainted in previous styles of green and cream, including open-top 706 and restored Balloon 700, complete with lining and municipal crests. In recent times frame joints of two of the historic cars with wooden bodies – Box 40 and Standard 147 – have been treated with fillings to stem leaking, followed by painting in their traditional livery, varnishing and lining-out. Today advertising on buses and trams is applied in vinyl, and several Balloons are finished in white to provide the background. Trams are brought into the Paint Shop to dry out before the painting work starts. Interior saloons of traditional trams used to be finished in dark oak, subsequently brightened to lighter shades, but today differing finishes are used.

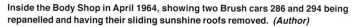

Inside the Body Shop in April 1964, showing two Brush cars 286 and 294 being repanelled and having their sliding sunshine roofs removed. *(Author)*

An interesting scene in the Body Shop on 10th September 1997 showing Trailer 681 after a fairly severe corner impact, and 707 being rebuilt in a new flat fronted 'Millennium' style.

(Below) More recent scenes in the Body Shop, in April 2002, showing Balloon 718 having been rebuilt in this form, along with Centenary 643 in the dramatically revised appearance. (Author, both)

As a completion to the refurbishment a tram may receive new indicator blinds prepared here, and fitted with restored seating with moquette by a specialist firm elsewhere. When the tram is towed back to the depot it indicates that it has been subjected to the skill of the painters, bodybuilders and fitters during its overhaul.

The story of the centralisation would not be complete in retrospect without the Blundell Street depot epilogue. On Good Friday 1964, this depot was brought back into use again as a running shed, and double-deck cars left this depot for Promenade duties via the long-disused line in Princess Street. Apparently, this proved too much for the residents, whose peace was shattered by rumbling trams on the doorstep again, after an absence of many years. Their objections were sustained, and the Transport Chairman agreed with them and promised an alternative arrangement for the trams. Consequently, work began on constructing a new outlet for tramcars at the Rigby Road entrance to the depot. Meanwhile, a number of trams were stranded in the building at Whitsuntide, which made it necessary for the temporary re-opening of Bispham Depot on Sunday, in order to run the open Boat cars. All the trackwork leading to the new entrance was

VARIED SCENES IN THE PAINT SHOP

Above: Numbers 718 and 643 again on 27th May 2002, with ladders and wheeled-gantries ready for painting the large side of the Balloon.

Below: In December 2005, 147 is seen drying out before rubbing down takes place. Also Box 40 in the same month, being partially repainted and varnished, showing Ray painting black over a template for the traditional lettering 'BLACKPOOL & FLEETWOOD'. *(Author)*

(Above) A scene in Blundell Street Depot at Easter 1964, showing Balloon 262, Standards 158 and 159 and Railcoaches, looking north towards the old entrance and ambulances.

(Centre) Interesting storage for trams 282, 170 and 147, the Lost Childrens' bus, and Maley & Taunton wheel and bogie sets.

(Below) August 1964, with a line of Boats, 267, Hovertram and Standard 48. The litter on the floor comes from trams that have been swept-out after being in use. (Author, all)

completed by the last week in June, and this was necessary for trams to cross the busy Rigby Road. When the overhead wiring was connected, it was pleasing to see that use had been made of the 'five-way' frog to the new entrance, although only four tracks were connected to the new approach. Provision for emergency exit through the old entrance was retained on tracks 1 and 2. When the power was switched on during the 3rd July, it was strange to see the Western Train disappearing in reverse through the new doorway, while the anxious eyes of the engineers watched the clearance at each side. The trolley dipped gracefully under the low portal – originally designed for buses – and the operation was complete, making a new lease of life for the original depot. This new approach was more convenient than the old, enabling cars to use Hopton Road and Lytham Road to enter service more quickly. The Chief Engineer at the time – Eric Kay – was pleased that it made it possible to use this depot for storing illuminated cars, trailers and 8ft wide Coronations, which were previously prevented from entering by the narrowness of the old doorway. Blundell Street depot was also used for storing equipment for the permanent-way, together with Works car 259 and trailer 260. Since the depot was also used by ambulances, a partition was made halfway down the depot. Unfortunately, a gale in 1982, blowing through open doors at each end, damaged the roof-supports holding the partition, and so a decision was made by the Borough to demolish the building. Today, on the car park, former depot track can be seen and it may be in the future that a new depot will be built on this site.

With the completion of the centralisation programme in 1964, it was very evident that much-needed economies had been effected. Efficiency on the maintenance of the tram fleet, together with new development, ensured that the remaining inter-urban Blackpool and Fleetwood service continued during the 20th Century. After 40 years of the present Works, it remains to be seen as to whether it will be reorganised once again to facilitate servicing new articulated trams, if they manifest themselves on a grant. However, 'Behind the Scenes' has shown the effective reputation of the Works in maintaining and enhancing trams in an aged fleet. This ensures that trams still maintain their status as one of the famous attractions of Blackpool.

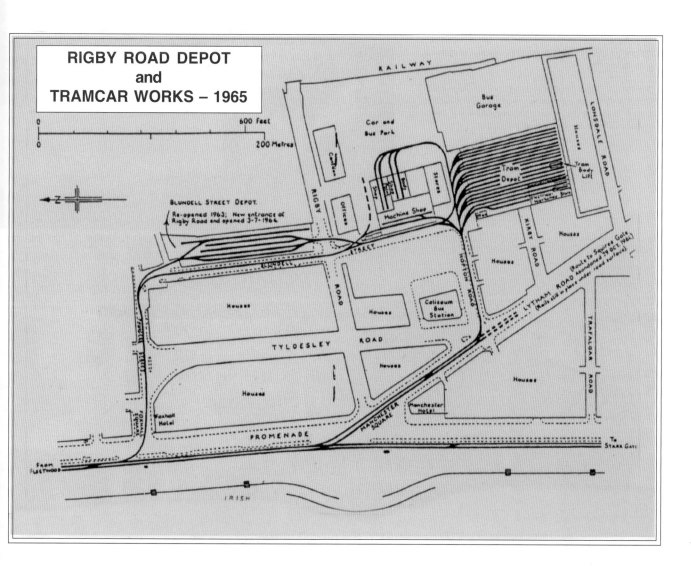

(Above) Television trams 166 and 165 in Princess Street, outside the old entrance to the Depot in 1965.

(Centre) An unidentified pair of cars, an English Electric Railcoach and a Boat, gleam in the evening sunshine outside the offices.

(Below) Western Train reversing past the Transport Office towards the new entrance of Blundell Street depot. This was the first tram in July 1964, and I was lucky to be able to record it. *(Author, all)*

A delightfully colourful picture with 59 in the imposing doorway of the historic depot, surmounted by 'CORPORATION TRAMWAYS', after a tour by the Fylde Tramway Society in May 1982. Today the stone sign is mounted outside the Transport Office.

Inside the depot, 59 is having its decoration finished as the *Daily Mirror Tram* in 1964. Boats and Hovertram 735 can also be seen. *(Author, both)*

Blackpool Corporation Transport

NOTICE TO PASSENGERS

INTRODUCTION OF ONE–MAN OPERATED VEHICLES

LOOK FOR THE
GOLDEN YELLOW AND
CRIMSON SINGLE DECK
PAY AS YOU ENTER

ONE–MAN OPERATED TRAMS

PASSENGERS ARE REQUESTED TO NOTE THAT WHEN ONE–MAN OPERATED VEHICLES ARE OPERATING ON THIS SERVICE, ATTENTION IS DRAWN TO THE FIVE POINTS LISTED BELOW, AND YOUR CO–OPERATION IS REQUESTED.

1. PLEASE SIGNAL THE DRIVER TO STOP IN GOOD TIME.
2. PAY THE DRIVER AS YOU ENTER.
3. HAVE THE EXACT FARE READY IF YOU CAN.
4. SIGNAL IN GOOD TIME WHEN YOU WISH TO ALIGHT.
5. ENTER BY THE FRONT DOOR, ALIGHT FROM THE CENTRE DOOR.

SEE FARE LIST OVERLEAF

TRANSPORT OFFICES.
BLUNDELL STREET.
BLACKPOOL.
MAY 1973

J. C. FRANKLIN,
GENERAL MANAGER.

POINTS TO NOTE

1 Please signal the driver to stop in good time

2 Pay the driver as you enter

3 Have the exact fare ready if you can

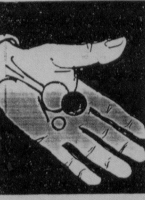

4 Signal in good time when you wish to alight

STOP

5 ENTER — FRONT DOOR
ALIGHT — CENTRE EXIT

A familiar sight on the Central Prom in 1976 with OMO 4 in the red livery and the Tower top painted for the Queen's Silver Jubilee. *(Jim Ingham)*

The OMO Cars Help The Tramway To Survive 1967-1984

The pruning of the tramway system in the early 'sixties created shock waves which continued to reverberate round the Transport Department throughout the decade. It seemed that no sooner had one crisis been overcome, than another loomed large on the horizon. Financial affairs played a large part in the fortunes of the tramway: its profitability – or otherwise – determining its success in the eyes of local government. When in 1967 a modest profit of £6,000 became a loss of £41,000, exacerbated by loan repayment charges of £29,000. In addition, voices were raised against continuing tramway operation in Blackpool. In contrast, the comparative profitability of the buses – £61,000 in 1968 – provided the anti-tram lobby with a feasible alternative. Surely – they argued – the financial plight of the Transport Department would be eliminated if the loss-making trams were replaced with profitable buses? The Promenade tramway could be converted into a bus-way, possibly funded by a 75% grant, which at that time was available from the Government for new road schemes. In January 1969, when a vote was taken in the Council Chamber about the future of the tramway, only two members of the Transport Committee voted against future tramway operation, and thus, fortunately, the trams were reprieved for the future.

The financial background to these periodic crises of confidence was a loss of passengers amounting to half a million between the years 1966 and 1975, equivalent to one-third of the total users. However, this was not exclusive to Blackpool's tramway, but was reflected in the entire passenger transport industry throughout Britain. The growth in car ownership and their use for daily travel to and from work, coupled with a drop in evening traffic, which arose from the increasing national habit of television viewing, were the twin factors

chiefly responsible. At Blackpool, the problem was exacerbated by the heavy seasonal traffic on the tramway which necessitated maintaining a large fleet of trams for part-year use only. While peak summer services required as many as 60 trams, in winter no more than fifteen were in service at any time. The winter Fleetwood service used to boast two routes on a twelve minute headway to North Station and Starr Gate until 1963, thus providing a six-minute headway between the two towns. Subsequently, a fifteen-minute service on the coastal tramway was supplemented by a thirty-minute bus service to Cleveleys via Dickson Road. The former tram services to Marton and Squires Gate, replaced with bus services, told a similar story of general decline in passengers.

By 1968, when the buses started to lose money, the tram losses could not be viewed in quite the same way. Of course, there were special factors which added to the tram losses, notably the heavy loan charges which had resulted from the purchases of the 25 Coronations in 1952-4, which drained the fortunes of the Transport Department until 1968. It was all the more galling to the management when these expensive trams proved to be less serviceable than the pre-war cars which still carried the bulk of the traffic. The four-motor Coronation cars with their heavy power usage, elaborate electrical equipment and a heavyweight of 19 tons unladen, proved to be the Transport Department's albatross throughout the decade. The unpalatable truth dawned that these 25 post-war tramcars, instead of providing the basis of future tramway operation, must be restricted to summer season only from 1964. Also, it was decided in that year to remove the Vambac equipment and replace it with conventional controllers, commencing with 323. Clearly, the Coronations just added to the problems of the Transport Department during a period of severe economic and political pressure. In retrospect, it can be understood why the 25 Coronations have not survived into the 21st century!

The changes in holiday patterns arising from cheap package holidays abroad also affected British resorts, including Blackpool, and was seen in the closure of Central Station in 1964. Accompanying the decline in tram passengers – from 3.3 million in 1959 to 1.2 million in 1970 – was the rise in crew costs, which had already rendered obsolete most of Blackpool's 48-seat trams and 56-seat buses. When the street tramways were replaced by buses in the early 'sixties opportunity was taken to buy 71-seat Leyland MCW Orions, which offered greater economy of operation. The seasonal tram fleet of double-deckers had their seating capacity increased by ten seats, while the 114-seat Twin-cars were double-ended. By the late 'sixties the rise in costs meant that more drastic measures had to be undertaken. Since most of the tram fleet needed the use of conductors, a new direction was sought. In 1968, one of the pre-war Railcoaches, 618, was lengthened to increase its seating capacity to 56 – like a Coronation – but this was insufficient to reduce operational costs, and the car remained unique.

In 1969, following the order for AEC Swift one-man buses, the concept of one-man operated trams was mooted for the first time. General Manager JC Franklin commented: "If I had tried to build a one-man tram in 1958 it wouldn't have stood an earthly, but after one-man buses had been introduced the climate was different". Accordingly, a 1937 Brush railcar, 638, was adapted to have a front entrance, using the existing centre doors as an exit. Unlike the 618 experiment, the rebuilding was fairly minimal with the removal of front partitions and the moving of the resistances to the roof within the trolley gantry.

(Facing page, upper) In April 1964, the first re-equipped Coronation 323 at North Pier seen in subdued livery. (Author)

(Facing page, lower) The trial-run for 618 at Fleetwood Ferry, showing its 49ft length and driven by Chief Engineer Alan Williams. (Author)

(Right) All-cream Brush car 638, showing the wrong destination going south and the driver seemingly talking to the conductress. Could there be a connection between these two comments? (John Fozard)

Painted all-cream, in keeping with one-man buses, this tram was doomed to failure. The modest rebuilding had given the car a too-narrow front entrance, situated behind the driver so making the fares difficult to collect, and, therefore, was condemned by the Transport Union at the outset. Joe Franklin subsequently described this car as a "false start", and 638 spent most of its time in the depot, or operated as a conventional car with a conductor. Eventually, the front door was removed although the driver's cab remained open and it retained its cream livery until 1973. Despite this false start, the General Manager clearly saw the one-man tram as the answer to their light traffic winter tram service, and he was determined to try again.

Following the favourable vote on the future of tramway operation in Blackpool at the beginning of 1969, an all-party Committee was set up in 1970 with the express purpose of examining the future operation of the tramway system. Mr Franklin remained convinced that the tramway was still the best means of transport along Blackpool Promenade to Fleetwood. He sought to present a reasoned case for more economical operation in the future, based on one-man trams for the winter service. Proposals for curtailing the tramway at Thornton Gate – or even Little Bispham – and relegating its role to a purely seasonal

attraction, were all considered by the Transport Committee. It became apparent that if a tramway system was to be continued at all, there was a lower limit of operations below which the capital expense could not be justified. The Fleetwood route provided a reason for the tramway, not only as a link between the two towns, but as a popular ride in the season, without which there could be a serious loss of revenue. Expenditure saved by restricting the mileage would be far outweighed by the loss of revenue, and the remaining few trams would still need the supporting services of depot, works, track-work and electrical supply. The Transport Department argued that for modest investment, taking into account a possible grant from the Ministry of Transport for conversion of tramcars to one-man operation, the tramway system could be run economically in the off-season. Thus, the unique tramway facility could be maintained ready for the heavy seasonal traffic.

The Department won the day, and in 1972 the Manager was quoted as saying: "Tramcars are part of the Blackpool scene, as a means of unhindered transport along the Promenade, they cannot be equalled. During extensive investigations which have taken place over a lengthy period, no obvious alternative form of passenger transport has become apparent for Blackpool Promenade in particular, and the Fleetwood route in general." The General Manager fought hard and continuously for a grant towards operating costs from the Rates Fund, and even though a large proportion of the Council agreed, a grant was never made. The battle to maintain the tramway in operation had been a long and hard one, and it remained for the Transport Department to prove that continued tramcar operation would be no more expensive than the alternative. Because of the unhappy

Three views of OMO 1 under construction:

(Above) The new wooden frame extension to the body upon the metal frame, recessed for the step and supported temporarily by wooden props.

(Centre) Side view showing the controller set along the tapering side, and the sliding window for the driver, replacing the opening windscreen.

(Lower) Looking through the windscreen frame along the 49ft saloon, with the centre platform raised and side steps for exits. The handbrake wheel and air brake column can be seen in the centre at the front. *(Author, all)*

experience with the prototype one-man car, 638, in 1969, the GM fully discussed the position with the Transport Union and decided that a Consultative Committee should be formed, which would meet regularly to be chaired by the Chief Engineer, Mr Alan Williams, and should include the Tramways Engineer, Eric Dyson, and representatives of the Union. Other senior members of the Electrical and Bodybuilding Sections also attended on most occasions, and the outcome of the planning was seen as a first-class team result.

Tests for clearance were carried out during 1971, using a Boat car rigged with a wooden frame at each end, to simulate the length of the new cars. It became obvious that a tapered-end would have to be incorporated in the new design, which would be more typical of Continental practice than had been traditional in Blackpool. The tapered ends thus restricted the space in the driver's cab, creating a problem of fitting the large EE Z-type controller. It had been hoped to use a modern lightweight controller, but the additional expense unfortunately precluded this, and the large controller had to be fitted on the right-hand side of the tapered end. This meant that the motorman was to drive with his right hand, breaking with a long-held tramway tradition. Right-handed operation was agreed with the Union before the design left the drawing-board, along with front position of handbrake and air brakes fittings, so that no practical problems existed. Once general acceptance of the design was gained, no time was lost in starting work.

It was estimated that a least nine cars plus spares would be needed to operate the basic winter service, and first into the Works bodyshop was 616 (269), closely followed by 620 (283). The ends of the cars were completely removed, and the bodies stripped down to the basic frame, allowing rewiring to take place as well as a complete overhaul of the bogies. Platform extensions were fitted to the ends of each car, and the side framework strengthened to carry the extra load created by the overhang of the new ends. The body design featured flush sides and roof, tapering at each end to a single windscreen width, surmounted by a destination indicator. The entrance door and two-step platform into the saloon occupied the full length of the tapered ends, and the existing centre doors were retained as exits. To facilitate movement along the saloon, the centre gangway was made level throughout, with two steps down to the centre-exit doors. The layout created a problem, in that the traditional tramcar reversible seats would not be practicable with a one-man vehicle, and longitudinal seats were not considered suitable for good visibility. Special back-to-back seat frames were fabricated and arranged in pairs except near the exits, where bench seats were used. With the 7ft 6in body this arrangement left a rather narrow gangway for passenger flow in a car whose capacity of 64 included 16 standing. A continuous grab-rail was fitted over the centre gangway, and the seats were fitted with grab-handles, while continuous strips for bell-signalling were installed over the windows. The whole car was panelled in aluminium, and presented a somewhat continental appearance apart from the trolley gantry, which unfortunately disclosed the car's origins!

More complete OMO 1 in January 1972 showing the off-side, tapering roof and diagonal-truss without the windscreen. (Author)

(Left) A new OMO tram on the Central Promenade in 1975. Outstanding in its new livery, number 2 has been fitted with an advertising-box.

(Facing page, upper) LOOK OUT – TRAMS ABOUT at Manchester Square in 1975, with OMO 7 loading and Boat 600 travelling north.

(Facing page, lower) OMO 7 and 618 standing adjacent in the depot electrical compound in 1975. Clearly 618 looks higher and wider than OMO 7. *(Author, all)*

By December 1971, the conversion programme was in full swing with two more cars – 220 (608) and 224 (610) – fully stripped in the depot, waiting for space in the Works. The use of Permanent-way car 5 (221) to become OMO 5 reflected the shortage of Railcoaches suitable for conversion. In the early 'sixties it had been the policy to break up the 1934 series of EE Railcoaches first, hence the few cars deemed suitable for this programme, which now included the works car and 220 saved for possible use as an illuminated feature car. These non-passenger fleet trams were used early in the programme, enabling other Railcoaches to be retained in service as long as possible. Consideration was given to eventually converting a total of 30 cars to one-man operation, which would have included the 1937 Brush cars, 17 of which remained in service. However, on closer examination, it was found that the Brush cars had underframes which would not easily lend themselves to extension and would have to be redesigned. This factor – together with the lightweight design of the EMB bogies – precluded their inclusion in the OMO programme. The benefit of hindsight showed that, with the only non-standard equipment of the thirties, the Brush cars would have been better candidates for first scrapping rather than the English Electric Railcoaches, 21 of which had disappeared in the early 'sixties. However, I should add that the motors and controllers of these cars were fitted to the Brush cars, which standardised then to a greater degree.

In April 1972, the first OMO car, 616, was rolled out of the paintshop for inspection by the press, in a striking new livery of sunshine-yellow with a crimson roof and doors. Apart from the special feature cars, this was the first change in livery since Railcoach 200 appeared in green and cream back in 1933. The aim was to make the one-man trams more easily recognisable for the travelling public, especially during the period of mixed operation with conventional Railcoach cars. With such a break from tradition, it was felt appropriate to start a completely new numbering system, hence the transfers were hardly dry on 616 before it was renumbered as 1. Subsequent trams followed in the series, until number 13 was reached, giving most of these cars their third fleet number since the fleet was renumbered in 1968. The new OMO 1 was inspected by Lt Col McNaughton of the Ministry of Transport, who drove it all the way to Fleetwood and found the new livery "very striking". He also stated that he considered the modified tramcar excellent, and was most impressed by the standard of workmanship throughout.

One-man tramcar service was to start after the 1972 Illuminations on the Fleetwood route, and by August OMOs 1–4 were lined up in Rigby Road depot all ready to enter service. Preparations on the route included the modification of shelters and queue barriers, changing the direction of loading in order to face passengers towards the front entrance of the new cars, and extension of paved areas at the stops to accommodate this.

The traditional 'Polo' tram-stop signs began to disappear in favour of queue boards, while in Fleetwood the number of town-centre stops were reduced to minimise traffic congestion. The public was prepared for the innovation with an attractive leaflet – designed by the Traffic Department – showing one of the new trams in a cartoon and demonstrating how 'they cannot work without your help'. The new service was due to operate with a 12-minute headway and had a simplified fare structure, which was printed on the leaflet. Since there would only be four OMO cars ready in time, conventional crewed cars would be alternated in service, which would ease the transition for the public.

The introduction of these new trams – OMOs as they became generally known – presented a different staffing problem to that experienced on the OMO buses in 1969, when volunteers had been sought to operate them. With the trams, it was necessary to train the older drivers first, otherwise their jobs would disappear as the change to one-man operation progressed. In order to give them the experience of handling the ticket machine and giving change, several of the new cars were given trial operational runs along the Promenade during the season. There were teething troubles at first, since the public were unaccustomed to having their money ready, and the drivers were unfamiliar with handling decimal coinage. Often the crewed cars followed the one-man trams in convoy, and it became necessary for the former to miss stops to avoid delays in service. This problem was faced on the Fleetwood route after the Illuminations, and it was necessary to increase the running time between Fleetwood and Starr Gate. Despite the initial difficulties and the 20% bonus paid to drivers of one-man vehicles, the new mode of operation saved money, eliminating 170 conductors' jobs since 1969 when OMO operation was first introduced on buses.

Back in the Workshops, the rebuilding programme – which had remained static during the summer period owing to pressure of accident repairs – resumed with OMO 5 (221) entering service during winter season. Two more cars, 617 and 619, which had been stripped in the depot during the summer and had their frames extended, went back into the Body Shop during the winter months for conversion to 6 and 7, and thus the momentum of the

(Left) Number 615 turning at Ash Street for Pleasure Beach, with the Balloon in service for Starr Gate.

(Below centre) Having crossed over the points is 615 with plastic tram 611 waiting to turn for Manchester Square. These cars became OMO 11 and 12 in 1975.

(Foot) Number 618 on the Fleetwood service at South Pier; notice the Coronation windscreen. *(John Fozard)*

(Facing page, upper) OMO 4 passing the original Tramroad shelter and about to traverse Rossall crossing. It still looks straight and unbowed in the red livery. *(Author)*

(Facing page, lower) A scene at Little Bispham in August 1977, as OMOs 6 and 7 turn for the Starr Gate service, while Balloon cars operate the Fleetwood service during the summer season. *(Author)*

programme resumed. Some of the cars selected for conversion were due for major overhaul, and others had been involved in accidents, necessitating rebuilding. An exception to the rule was 618 – the lengthened car – which was repaired in the Body Shop during the summer of 1972 after a crash, and continued in service until the end of 1975, becoming the 13th and final OMO conversion. Nineteen-seventy-three proved to be a vintage year at Blackpool, with seven OMO cars in service, along with final Railcoach 615, the two Hybrids, 611 – the plastic tram – 618, and the three towing cars – 678, 679 and 680 – which were now running singly again. Thus, the ubiquitous English Electric Railcoach could be seen running in five different guises that season. Also, 6 and 7 were fitted with advertising boxes on their roofs, taken from Coronations which had been withdrawn. The remaining five Coronation cars made occasional appearances on the Promenade as 'specials', while the double-deckers had taken over the Fleetwood service from 1st July. The OMO cars were restricted by agreement from running in Fleetwood during the busy season and spent most of their time on the Little Bispham and Starr Gate service during the day from 9am to 6pm, after which they went on to the Fleetwood route. The conversion programme subsequently produced 8 and 9 in 1974 and 10, 11, 12 followed in 1975, which allowed the Works to service other cars at the same time. The slowing down of the OMO programme took account of the 'human factor' in the Transport Department. There were a number of tram conductors who had never done bus work, and for whose benefit two-man trams continued to operate during the winter season. Gradually, retirement and retraining reduced their numbers to one tram-crew by 1975. That season, Driver Lascelles and Conductor Hollingsworth staffed the one remaining crew operated tram in service until December, after which they retired and the tram route became fully one-man operated for the first time.

Changes at the top were soon to have a far-reaching effect on the tramway. The architects of the OMO programme, in the form of General Manager JC Franklin and the Chief Engineer AH Williams, had both left the Department by Easter 1974. Mr Franklin retired after 20 years of keeping the trams on the road – an

achievement which will be to his lasting credit – and was succeeded by Mr DL Hyde, the Coventry Manager. Alan Williams, who had taken-up an appointment in South Africa, had been succeeded by Mr Stuart Pillar, the Deputy Manager and Engineer at Preston. The new team was able to take a fresh look at the situation, now that some experience following the changes had been gained on the tramway. The trams themselves, while successful in service, had many shortcomings which needed investigation. Superficially, the most apparent was the deterioration of the new 'plum and custard' livery, which looked somewhat drab after exposure to the salt air and sand of the Promenade. However the sagging of the new body-ends, constantly needing straightening by bracing the body-frame, indicated that the mounting of the bogies should have been moved outwards to support the additional length.

With the number of OMO cars in service, some very high mileages were reached by the new cars. OMO 1 had operated 44,000 miles in 7½ months, while the average of 35,000 miles far exceeded that of the conventional cars. Some technical difficulties were becoming apparent with the running gear, and the sagging car bodies already mentioned due to increased length with the heavy loadings on the Promenade. Loads and body movements about the original wheelbase were affecting tyre-life on the bogies. An investigation was undertaken and the coventional primary suspension of leaf-springs was replaced by 'Metalastic' rubber suspension, similar to that used on London Transport Underground stock and many Continental trams. OMO 10, in the new red and cream livery, was the first to be modified, making its test run on 17th January 1975, and was soon named 'Bouncing Bessie' by the crews because of its jogging motion. Numbers 11 and 12 followed by May and June 1975 in the new livery, but the trolley tower of 12 was painted red and not cream like 10 and 11. Modifications followed to the bogies and by 1976 six OMO cars were equipped with the new suspension, resulting in improved riding qualities.

Meanwhile, preparations had been under way during 1974 for a limited experiment with a modern pantograph collector, which at that time was being developed by Brecknell Willis for the American Boeing Corporation's light rail articulated cars for Boston and San Francisco. In April 1974 overhead-line car 754 was fitted with a modern frame to investigate what work would be necessary to re-align the overhead to cope with a pantograph, especially round curves and turning circles. Later, 754 was fitted with a pantograph for trials and in June 1975 the oldest car in the fleet – originally 31 – made a test run to Fleetwood, looking somewhat incongruous. A month later on 3rd July, towing-car 678 went into service between Little Bispham and Starr Gate fitted with the Brecknell Willis pantograph, which could be raised and lowered from the driver's cab. This car ran throughout the season without undue incident; a buzzer in the cab warned the driver of any snag which made the pantograph lose contact with the overhead line. This was only a preliminary trial, and more followed in 1976.

(Facing page) Two red cars at Bispham in 1978, with Dreadnought 59 on a tour, and OMO 8 on service to Starr Gate, with a Boat about to go astern in between them.

(Above) A striking view at Harrowside in October 1975, with Brush 625 passing OMO 5, and Balloons 708 and 707 following, during an LRTA tour.

(Right) May 1975, and a view showing OMO 5 in the new red livery, with two unidentified cars and the Tower seen from a Boat in 1981. More significantly, the car is now sporting a diamond format pantograph, eliminating the need for turning the trolleypole since the conductor has also been eliminated! (Author, all)

Local government reorganisation in April 1974 had given control over transportation in their area to County Councils, which in practice delegated to Borough Councils like Blackpool the day-to-day running of the services. Lancashire County Council then became involved in the Blackpool tramway directly for the first time. Its Transportation Committee voiced the opinion – at long last – that the Promenade tramway at Blackpool was an amenity which ought to be continued. It was thus to the County Council that the Transport Department looked for financing its next modernisation programme.

To the travelling public, the most obvious change to the OMO trams in 1975 was the new red and cream livery, first introduced on 10 and then all subsequent cars in the series. With their red roof, doors and dash-panel, the cars looked brighter and more distinctive than the original 'plum and custard' livery, the last of which – 9 – was repainted in August 1976. Real tests with the pantograph came in February 1976 when OMO car 5 was fitted with the Brecknell Willis unit, followed by cars 4 and 13 later in the year. The fact that 5 and 13 were subsequently refitted with trolley-poles by the year end would indicate that there had been some problems which would have to be rectified. However, only 618 had remained for conversion to complete the initial batch of one-man trams and in spring 1976 emerged as OMO 13, with the added sophistication of fluorescent lighting and a trolleybus alternator. It went out on trial with the alternator on the platform in June 1976, and sadly the former melted at Gynn Square. An alternator from the former Walsall trolleybus system was fitted above the platform later in June 1976. However, this completed the planned programme, enabling a full winter service to be operated by the OMO cars.

On 16th August in that year, Coronation 660 remained the only one in the fleet, since 663 was bought by Graham Oliver and 655, 661 and 662 were removed for scrapping. Following the demise of the 25 Coronations,

Seen from the Blackpool Belle on a tour, is OMO 5 fitted with the alternative Brecknell Willis collector arm and approaching a Balloon in service on the facing track. Notice the Space Tower of the Pleasure Beach. *(Author)*

by the end of 1976 the 27 double-deckers remained the largest single class of trams left in the fleet. Two of their number – 714 and 725 – had been derelict in Blundell Street depot for a number of years, since they needed to be completely rebuilt, and additional labour was not available.

Lack of further suitable trams for conversion to OMOs, without sacrificing the trailer towing-cars 678 to 680 or the open Boat cars , together with the inherent disadvantages of the design, indicated the need for a new direction for the fleet modernisation programme. The problem with the double-deckers had always been their slow loading and heavy crew costs of three. Chief Engineer Stuart Pillar began working on a design for a prototype front entrance double-deck car, which could be used with one conductor or as a one-man car. This would gain the maximum flexibility in operation by doubling the capacity or halving it immediately, which would save labour costs and increase productivity. Work began on 725 during 1976, involving extensive alteration of the underframe, increasing its length to 46ft and increasing the wheelbase. The lessons of the single-deck OMO cars had been learned, and there would be no need for a tapered end which resulted in loss of space. The new design incorporated a full width front, with a wide doorway opposite the driver and 90° stairs immediately behind the driver's cab. Wide panoramic windows for the saloons would give good all round viewing for the passengers. Technical innovations included Metalistik suspension, modern control equipment and a pantograph collector, making 725 (renumbered 761) the most modern double-decker anywhere in the world. If successful, it was planned that 761 would become the first of a new fleet, maintaining Blackpool's place as a tramway pioneer, but we shall see how it evolved in the next chapter.

(Above) A nostalgic scene on Central Promenade as OMO 1 passes Blackpool Belle 731 on its tour on 21st April 1979. Enthusiast David Evans is one of several people photographing it. *(Author)*

(Below) OMO 12 in the depot between OMO 5 and Boat 605 all fitted with trolleys. *(Jim Ingham)*

Number 761, completed and looking striking in its new-style livery on 19th April 1979, before leaving the Paint Shop. *(Author)*

Jubilee Cars 761 & 762
– A New Generation For Double-Deckers?

After four years of rumour and speculation, on 19th April 1979 Blackpool's new double-deck tram emerged from the paint shop to reveal its appearance for the first time. Since this was merely shunting to the fitting shop, the audience was restricted to a few workmen, platform staff and by chance your author! My first impression was one of length, accentuated by the striking livery of parallel green and cream lines of the Atlantean bus livery. The similarity with a modern bus was so great that one of the platform staff was heard to say: "When that gets to Talbot Square, the time keeper will probably send it to Layton on a number 5!" The complete transformation from pre-war Balloon 725 left no clue as to its previous identity, in effect it was a completely new tram numbered 761. The similarity to a bus was not accidental, since 761 had been created from components used in bus-building, including windows, seats, handrails, windscreens and lights. The rebuilding was not merely a cosmetic exercise, for the control equipment and running-gear also marked a radical departure from the past. The impact of the new car was as great as the first Coronation car in 1952, and to associate it with another royal occasion, the Transport Department christened 761 as its 'Jubilee Car'.

Its creation had not been easy, arising as it did from the conviction that the Transport Department needed a new all-purpose tram for summer and winter operation, with the enhanced capacity provided by a double-decker. Experience with the thirteen one-man cars showed that more advanced design techniques were needed to give rebuilt cars a longer life. The one-man cars had proved entirely successful in operation, but structurally were not withstanding the heavy loadings experienced on the Promenade. The 27 Balloons were disused for nearly half of the year and had not shared the heavy service conditions of the single-deck fleet. Two of these cars – 714 and 725 – had been withdrawn for some years and stored in Blundell Street depot, and it was 725 which was the first chosen for rebuilding. The concept of the new car, as revealed by drawings produced in 1975, was a front-loading tram capable of one-man operation in winter and off-peak periods, while offering a high seating capacity with good viewing for the passengers. The double-deck Balloons had, by union agreement, been operated by two conductors, owing to the centre-entrance with its large folding platform doors and twin staircases. This expensive crewing would be eliminated on the new car, and, incidentally, solve the annual problem created by the departure of seasonal student labour before the end of the Illuminations. Technically, the new car would provide an opportunity to experiment with different control equipment and develop the rubber chevron suspension which was successfully used on the OMO cars. This time an opportunity was taken to break away from the heavy dc controller, and new lightweight low-voltage controllers had been considered for this car. Discussions took place with Westinghouse – a major electrical equipment manufacturer – about this provision.

Work commenced in earnest on 26th October 1976, when the shell of 725 entered the Body Shop. The complete ends of the car were removed, and the floor was lifted to allow extensive alterations to the main frame. Experience with the single-deck OMO cars had shown the mistake of leaving the bogies in the same position, when the length of the cars had been extended to 49ft. The length of the new car was to be extended to 46ft, and the wheel-base extended from 19ft 6in to 22ft 4in. The frame extension allowed a full-width body at the ends with a 4ft 8ins entrance and therefore, a more spacious platform than had been possible on tapering cars 1–13. The teak framework of the existing body was altered by the removal of the centre entrance and staircases, and the enlargement of the windows to take load-bearing metal window frames. Meanwhile, Metal Sections Ltd of Birmingham were constructing completely new metal-framed ends for the car, which would be attached to the existing teak body-frame at Blackpool. While the car body was taking shape during 1977, the bogies were undergoing an equally drastic rebuilding in the Fitting Shop. Primary 'Metalastik' suspension, which had increased the tyre life on the OMO cars to 100,000 miles, was incorporated along with the secondary rubber suspension, to give a softer ride and reduce maintenance costs. To eliminate the traditional brake linkage, new air operated spring parking brakes were fitted, together with separate air-operated brake cylinders on all eight wheels. By the end of 1977, work on the body of the car had stopped owing to financial restrictions, and so priority was given to the bogies.

In early 1978 the bogies were completed, and it was decided to test them under Balloon car 708, which went out on trial in February with the test equipment mounted in the saloon. Loading tests were carried out using piles of brake shoes to simulate full loads of passengers in the upper and lower saloons. It was found that the new bogies gave a fairly 'soft' ride, and therefore the car body was prone to rolling, and this was

Three Balloons, 706, 714 and 725, in Blundell Street depot in July 1971, all suspended from service. Each subsequently changed its appearance. *(Author)*

(Above) A contrast in appearance between 705 and 761, seen undergoing rebuilding in the Body Shop during 1978. The new end-section frame is impressive.

(Below) This scene in the Paint Shop enables us to compare 761 with the traditional Balloon.   All the equipment has been moved from the track ready for 761's departure 19th April 1979.

(Opposite) 761 being towed by the venerable Diamond-T into Hopton Road, prior to pushing it into the Fitting Shop. It is now clearly much longer than a Balloon car. *(Author all)*

attributed to the new suspension. Shortly after Easter the bogies were rolled under 761, trials for which would eventually follow. Meanwhile, problems with the supply of new control equipment led the department to reluctantly consider using the old dc controllers in their new tram. Fortunately, the Westinghouse Brake & Signal Company expressed an interest in developing, solid-state control system for 761, having seen the car under construction. Accordingly, an order was placed with Westinghouse for a 'chopper' control system. It was planned that the equipment would be located under the stairways, and driver operation would be by a 'joy-stick' mounted in the cab. By pushing the stick forward, the driver would select acceleration, and by pulling it back the air braking system would come into operation. It was not considered necessary to provide electric rheostatic braking, and the Department of Transport Railway Inspectorate gave a dispensation for 761 to be exempt from the legal requirements that this tram should have such braking. Discussions took place with the Railway Inspectorate on many facets of the tram, from the early stages of its design.

Since the new car was a prototype for Blackpool, discussions took place on the interior layout with the representatives of the platform staff. Originally, it had been planned to seat 110 passengers, but this was reduced to 100 by the use of single seats at the stair head and centre of the upper saloon, in order to improve passenger movement. Fixed bus-type seating was adopted in view of the intended one-man operation, with each side of the gangway facing in opposite directions, apart from the end two rows of seats upstairs, which faced outwards. This would give the passengers maximum choice and good visibility, without resorting to the highly unpopular back-to-back seats of cars 1 to 13.

Before the body could be fully completed, the electrical equipment had to be fitted, and the car moved to the depot electrical compound where there was a traction supply. Tests on the control equipment were carried out by Westinghouse during autumn 1978. Returning to the Body Shop on 23rd October 1978, work on the lower saloon and the driver's cabs was completed. Good visibility was to be a feature of the driving

position, with its adjustable pedestal seat similar to that of a bus. An impressive row of instruments, including a speedometer, faced the driver on a single console, with the control lever mounted on the right. Added refinements on this tram included an air-operated reset mechanism for the lifeguard and for lowering the pantograph collector, together with air-sanding equipment. On the roof a centrally-mounted dwarf pantograph of diamond profile was used, rather than the large single-arm Brecknell Willis type used on the OMO cars. Before painting, 761 looked very tall and slender from the front and massive from the side, but the new 'Atlantean' livery improved its proportions and gave it a distinctive appearance. Although two-and-a-half years may have seemed a long time for reconstruction, Chief Engineer Stuart Pillar was anxious to 'get it right' for the first time. Any mistakes could have proved not only costly but might have jeopardised the prospect of further new cars, so 761 had to be a success from the outset.

The painting completed and the pantograph mounted, 761 went on trials during May and June 1979, attracting public attention whenever it appeared. Some of the trials were carried out at night after the normal service had finished, and on one occasion an anxious moment occurred when 761 – with General Manager Derek Hyde at the controls – went 'dead' at the foot of Gynn hill. After a few minutes silence, the car started moving forward again as another tram passed on its way to the depot. An explanation was later found in the fact that the solid-state control equipment had been programmed for an overhead-line voltage of between 450 and 600 volts, while at night the Gynn sub-station was supplying 604 volts to its section, until another car passing through reduced it to below 600v, and thus enabled 761 to move again. Adjustments were subsequently made to allow for this unforseen situation. The critical test came on 7th June, when the Railway Inspector arrived to examine and report on this new car. Happily, he passed it for driver training, which commenced on 25th June. Finally, on 2nd July the new car went into service on the Fleetwood route. It was fitting that its first driver should have been the late Jim Ingham, who had been closely associated with the project as the trade union representative, and Chairman of the Fylde Tramway Society. Many firsts were to follow: the Civic launch by the Mayor on July 4th, and also the first hire to the FTS on July 8th.

(Above) Upper saloon of 761 showing the fixed seats with grab-rails, facing the opposite way on each side, and with stairways at each end, fitted with mirrors above. All rather bus-like.

(Facing page, upper) Cleveleys on 4th June 1979, with 761 on trial admired by a queue of passengers, but showing RESERVED. Doubtless their admiration would have been even greater had they been able to actually get on the tram! Notice the mini-pantograph raised by supports.

(Facing page, lower) Lower-saloon showing the large windows, fluorescent lights and good forward view from the nearside seats. By now most passengers would have become accustomed to a poor forward view on the off-side if they used modern double-deck buses whose staircases, of necessity, created a similar obstruction to passengers's vision. (Author all)

The general public liked the new double-deck car, as did the crew who operated it. Acceleration and braking were smooth, controlled by the 'chopper' system which eliminated the possibility of bad driving. Of course, drivers were specially trained for this differing technique from the conventional EE controllers. Riding was extremely steady on the newly relaid Promenade track south of Manchester Square, but could be lively when running light on the poorer sleeper track. Loading and unloading on the busy Promenade through the single doorway tended to be slower than the OMO cars with their separate entrance and exit. The provision of a roving conductor on the car to assist the driver collecting the fares helped the situation. Circulation at the foot of the stairs behind the driver was assisted by the removal of one seat at each end, reducing the seating capacity to 98 passengers. There were a few snags, possibly the most embarrassing being when 761's pantograph 'lost' the overhead at the depot doorway on its first outing. Alterations had to be made to the height of the overhead line at the depot entrance, and at several parts of the system. Also, on 20th June 761 hit the depot doors, since it was entering on the wrong track near to the door-frame, and in late August it was blowing switches. Westinghouse investigated this and changed the heated printed circuit tray, after which there were no more problems. This close liaison with Westinghouse during the early days, ensured a successful first season for the car. Chief Engineer Stuart Pillar now had plans to restore 714 in the same manner as 761.

Negotiations were started with the trade unions for one-man operation during the winter months and 14th January 1980 saw 761 in service on the Fleetwood route, achieving one of the original aims of the project: a large-capacity tram operated by the driver only. The large car provided useful extra capacity for the service, without the crush-loading of the single-deckers or the costly operation of the double-deckers with a crew of three.

Number 762 on its first trial run at Bispham on 1st April 1982, unpainted and showing the bogies without the lower panelling, in order to test their clearance on curves. The peaked domes replicate contemporary bus design fashion. *(Author)*

What of the future? 761 had been a success, and the experience gained would be used in designing a second prototype car from 714. Work started before the end of 1979 and 714 was back in Blundell Street depot early in 1980, with its ends removed, bracing struts fitted, stair-wells filled and the sliding roof removed, and with the solid roof completed. There was a significant difference in layout planned to improve passenger-flow on 762, including a centre-exit and centrally mounted stairways. This would enable the car to load and unload simultaneously, and so speed its operation in service. It was also felt that there should be more technical innovations to improve riding quality, and so a comparison of the two prototype 'Jubilee' cars would determine the future design of the double-deck fleet. Once again new ends were ordered, but this time 762 was also to have new bogie frames by Wickhams, using the existing wheels. Control equipment – as used on 761 – was in the balance, since Westinghouse had been taken-over by Brush and the price had doubled. Alternatives were thus sought, but by December 1980 a contract was signed with Brush to deliver the equipment in 6 months. Number 762 entered the Body Shop by December 1980, and early in 1981 work was progressing quickly with the two ends added. Stuart Pillar did tell me that progress followed a grant of £40,000 before the end of the financial year. Roof ribs were fitted to the ends and platforms were extended

View of the Metalastik bogies for 762 and Centenary cars, showing the rubber
inserts for the axle-boxes and the longer bogie-frame. *(Author)*

with the front doors. The seating plan for 90 would have seats facing the centre downstairs, thus encouraging people to move into the rear saloon, with luggage racks at the bottom of the stairs. The new bogies from Wickhams were assembled in Blackpool, with wider springing and shock-absorbers to stop the car rolling. By the end of 1981 all the top saloon was completed inside, outside panelling fitted, and the seats were in position. The first electrical equipment was installed, and the panels over the bogies were to be higher than those on 761, to ensure clearance at the curves.

Number 762 moved under its own power for the first time on 31st March 1982 from the Fitting Shop into Blundell Street for the formal presentations to Engineers Stuart Pillar and Eric Dyson upon their retirement. Its first day on the Promenade was in unpainted condition on 1st April, for testing stopping distances. I noticed that 762 still bounced like 761, but did not roll. Bogies were much longer, because of self-adjusting brake mechanisms at each end. Since the bogies projected out beyond the body-line of the car, the lower panels had not yet been fitted. Its pantograph was the one from OMO 13, suitably strengthened. With the bogie-centres of 5ft 6in, the sound of the wheel-beat was more even, somewhat like the Coronations.

Inevitably, this reconstruction would raise the question of new cars for the future of tramway operation in Blackpool. Early in 1983, 762 had proved very reliable and satisfactory in service, but more problems had been encountered with 761. Therefore, a new bogie set was ordered for 761 and consideration was given to future rebuilding of accident-damaged 705 and 706. In retrospect, it is ironic to find that 761 and 762 remain unique in the fleet, and maintain the winter service with eight Centenary cars. As the late Stuart Pillar subsequently said: "It has been a missed opportunity!"

An impressive view of 762, seen entering Albert Square in Fleetwood, looking imposing
in the traditional street scene and dwarfing the rest of the traffic. *(John Fozard)*

Postcript On The Balloons

The question remains as to the future of the double-decker Balloons when there was no further development of the Jubilee cars constructed from 714 and 725 after 1982. From the original 27 double-deckers – half enclosed from 1941/2 – one was lost in October 1982 when 705 was broken-up along with trailer 688 in Blundell Street depot, before the building itself was demolished. This resulted from the head-on collision with 706 in July 1980 when somebody had left the Pleasure Beach turning-circle points opened, and the southbound car unexpectedly turned right. However, 706 was fortunately restored as an open-topper for the Centenary in 1985, named 'Princess Alice' and this proved to be the best outcome from the unexpected collision. It was first fitted with a pantograph and had a short section of centre-roof over the stairways, but this had to be replaced with a traditional trolley which was safer for the open-top passengers. The novelty of riding on an open-topper was further revived with the presence of Dreadnought 59 from 1976 to 1990, and with its subsequent absence 706 provided the requisite satisfaction for visitors and enthusiasts. Incidentally, other open-toppers subsequently joined 706: diminutive Stockport 5 in 1996 and larger Marton 31 came from Beamish in Autumn 1997 for the Centenary of the Blackpool & Fleetwood Tramroad in 1998.

The upper view of 762 at Manchester Square in 1982 shows the striking appearance of the original livery.

A good comparison, below, between the original 724 in the 'eighties livery and 762, at North Pier in 1983, with a red OMO neatly framed between them. *(Author, both)*

(Upper) The end of Tram Sunday 2006, with 706 *Princess Alice* loading at Fisherman's Walk, Fleetwood, and looking handsome in its original livery, whilst also carrying number 243. *(Author)*

(Centre) Fleetwood Ferry in October 2004, with 700 in the wartime livery. The windscreen hoods have been wrongly-fitted to this series of ex-open-toppers but older members of the tramway fraternity will probably remember this colour scheme with a degree of affection. *(Author)*

(Lower) Number 712 at the Ferry in 2004, having been repainted in the post-war livery for the 70th Anniversary. Large cream trams can look very smart but there is no denying the fact that green paint hides the rust on the panels! *(Author)*

(Upper) Stripped down to its frame without the cab-front 700 looks forlorn on 17th February 1996.   Work to the frame has been done in the Fitting Shop. *(James Millington)*

(Lower) In the Body Shop, below centre, with the new panels, windows, indicator-frames and mock-ventilators – Autumn 1996. *(Author)*

Complete in the Paint Shop as the undercoating is taking place ready to restore the Balloon its original appearance. A line of these trams in the maker's factory in the 'thirties must have been an impressive sight.

(Facing page) A unique scene at North Pier on Good Friday 28th March 1997 showing 700 and 703, both in the wartime livery, but differing between indicator styles and method of power collection. The fluorescent yellow blinds add little to the effect. *(Author, both)*

Following the undoubted climax of the Tramway Centenary in 1985, the next development of the Balloons came in 1996 with the restoration of 700, which as 237 was originally the pioneer of streamlined open-toppers in 1934. Since 706 had been restored to its original open-top condition, it was decided that 700 should be restored as it had been enclosed in 1941/2. There was every desire to rebuild the car substantially, so it was stripped down to its teak frame without its frontage, apart from the front tapering frame of the upper deck. A strengthened front frame was fitted, thus enlarging the driver's cab with twin windscreens and a pair of indicators above, so restoring its original appearance. Along the side, the saloon windows were fitted with half-drop windows complete with glass louvres and a row of imitation ventilators above them. While modern shatterproof glass had to be fitted, the upper-deck curved ones remained original plate glass. Internally, the saloons were restored with a simulated non-slip surface, with a mottled brown walking strip, and coloured green under the seats. Traditional reversible seats with green patterned moquette were fitted to both saloons, and the woodwork was restored to its original varnished dark brown appearance. The ceilings resemble the original Alhambrinal panelling using fibreglass, although it was possible to remove such original panelling from some of the other Balloons. The lighting recreates the original glass tinted shades, and the EE Z6 controllers had the gleaming chrome surface restored in the driver's cabs. The side indicators permanently show PROMENADE, while the original metallic number 237 is fixed above the centre doors. The livery is traditional green, relieved by cream lines at three levels sweeping down to flares at each end, strikingly featuring the tapering V pointing down to the centre buffer. Happily, 700 was equipped with its trolley, and the headlamps retain their external appearance with halogen lights fitted. This meets the needs of service car drivers at night, to see the track throughout the northern rural section of the tramway. While the restoration of an historic Balloon was desirable, it qualified for service, and so it has been seen regularly on the Starr Gate and Fleetwood service during the summer season. However, after dewiring its trolley fairly regularly, it met its Waterloo on Good Friday 2005, when its trolley dewired after Rossall Beach and swung round to penetrate the bracket-arm which broke it off. Having been towed back to the depot, 700 was then fitted with a pantograph for safety, but the assurance was made that it would be fitted with a trolley for special occasions. Consequently, it so appeared with 706 on 10th July VE and VJ Day and also Tram Sunday 2005. Apart from this, it has to be said that the striking appearance of 700 ensures that it portrays the origins of a Blackpool double-decker of the 'forties. Thus it enhances the historical tradition of the tramway, standing out amongst advert-covered Balloons. When number 717 was restored in 2006 it was fitted with a new underframe but should represent the second series of Balloons in the 'thirties livery, with front twin-indicators, metallic windscreens and half-drop windows, together with Alhambrinal panelling. Thus, the original 27 double-deckers will be represented by three cars of original styles. Sadly, the sunshine sliding roofs and lifeguards will not be restored on 717, because of the changed 21st Century safety requirements.

In contrast to three double-deckers in their original appearance, the four rebuilt Balloons, partially resembling the shape of Jubilee cars, do not have modified passenger-flow doors and modern equipment. In August 1998, rebuilt 707 went into service with a vertical flat-front – losing the original raked front – modern

The complete body-frame of 718 seen in the Body Shop during August 2000, the original teak frame having been extended by a metal frame in the new style. *(Author)*

front lights, and windows fitted with an inward-opening top-section. At first, the front upper-deck curved windows were not fitted – as later seen on 709 – and this was said to reduce its likeness to the rear of an Atlantean bus. The driver's cab had a fixed windscreen, no outer door, and air-conditioning which did not function, so that drivers complained of feeling faint in the cab. Accordingly, a small opening section had to be fitted to the side window. In the saloons fixed seating was used – half facing in each direction – but there was insufficient leg-room between the seats. The forward view in the upper-deck was improved, but the big disadvantage was that the crew of three had to be maintained, because of the traditional location of two staircases down to the centre platform. At the time, I asked the engineers why the style of the front entrance and centre-exit could not be adopted for 707. The answer was simply that the cost of returning to the design and equipment of the Jubilees would be too great. However, 707, 709, 718 and 724 could have a front entrance, retain their traditional controllers fitted on the right side like the OMOs, and thus reduce the need for an extra crew-member.

The Millennium style of livery in green and cream also had matt-black round the new windows and a grey skirt. The indicator panel was large and quite striking, and later was fitted to 761 and 762. Number 724 was chosen because its underframe was rotten, and it was proposed to fit a new one. In November 2000, the body-lift at the end of track 11 separated the teak body of 724 by lifting it from the underframe, which was removed and replaced by a new one, with the body lowered onto it. There had been a delay in completing the rebuilding because of the preoccupation of restoring Standard 147 and creating Trawler Cevic 633 during 2001. Number 718 had been completed before then and had joined 707 and 709, which, in 2005, were covered with advertising liveries, 709 having a scrambled version of 'Sea Life'. However, I feel that they are somewhat inadequate, bearing in mind the success of 761 and 762 in 1982, 20 years before. With 713 restored on a new underframe in 2005, retaining its original appearance apart from the frontal skirt lowered in the absence of the lifeguards, we have 20 Balloons of 1934, of which three are restored to their original appearance, and four Millennium rebuilt types. Ultimately, the verdict will depend upon future developments, including the legal requirements for access of the disabled, but I feel that if there are new low-floor articulated trams to maintain the principal service with easy access, the Balloons should be retained for seasonal popular transport for the general public. Undoubtedly, the streamlined Balloons have been an essentially successful class of trams for over 70 years and we must hope they will be with us for many more years to come.

(Upper) In the Body Shop, in 1999, 709 is seen almost complete, being fitted with new windows, and now having been painted in the new-style livery with dark skirt.

(Centre) The final Millennium 724 seen below in Cleveleys Square, and here demonstrating its great length, in April 2004. It is finished in the Metro-style livery.

(Lower) Rebuilt 713 is seen at the foot of the page. Not visible, of course, is its new underframe in this view at Fleetwood Ferry in October 2005. Finished in the plain white colour scheme, the lower front skirt should in fact be matt-black, like 709 above. *(Author, all)*

A New Generation – The Centenary Cars

The expense of the Jubilee cars undoubtedly explains why no further examples of this type were built. However, by 1983 the condition of the drooping OMO cars was creating urgent problems. Transport Manager Derek Hyde, and the new Engineer Bernard Brown, therefore saw that the priority should be to replace them with some new single-deck cars. Undoubtedly, the development of Jubilee car 762 pointed to Wickham bogies and electrical equipment by Brush. The Balloons, therefore remained in traditional form, while it was planned to have ten new single-deck cars built with similar technical specification as 762. 7th January 1983, was the date when tenders for a prototype tram were to be submitted, and they were expected from Leyland, East Lancs Coachbuilders, Metro-Cammell and Duple Coachbuilders. Manager Derek Hyde said that control equipment would probably be mounted on the roof with a dwarf tower on the top – reminiscent of the Coronations! The car would be 49ft long 8.25ft wide, and the old wheelsets would be used in the interests of standardisation in the tram fleet. It was expected that two more bogie sets by Wickhams would be ordered – one for 761 and one for the new tram. The press reported that the tender from East Lancs Coachbuilders was £59,000 for the body and £27,000 for the electrical equipment. As part of the body design, the centre-exit doors would be off set, allowing the driver to be able to observe passengers leaving the tram. In June 1983 the new bogies were in the Works Fitting Shop, assembled with the wheels, but without the brake-mechanism, and this was labelled as for new car number 21. Later in the year there was some delay in the assembling of the body underframe, and it was confirmed that the body would have windows like Atlantean buses, but there would be no curved roof-lights like the Railcoaches. The new tram would have illuminated advertising boxes, surmounted by a tower for the pantograph. The total cost was deemed to be £138,000 – as against £330,000 for a continental Duewag car. The plan was for the new prototype tram to be in operation in 1984, with a further three cars in each of the three following years, totalling ten. OMOs would then be scrapped, as they were replaced by the new trams. News then came that the new tram would not be numbered 21, but that it would have three-digit number 641 – a familiar combination today.

An unusual sight of a tram on a low-loader as 641 is seen *en-route* from East Lancashire Coachbuilders at Blackburn on the A59 to Blackpool. Note that the picture shouts 'made in Lancashire' – in addition to the tram, the tractor of the articulated rig is an Atkinson, from Walton-le-Dale, and the company owning it and entrusted with the move is Preston-based. Who will deliver the next generation of trams, on what, and from where? *(Author)*

In the Fitting Shop, 641 has been mounted on its new bogies. Though it has not yet gained its pantograph tower, it still looks handsome. *(The Gazette)*

I remember seeing plans at that time for the new car, and it seemed to look somewhat like the German Stadtbahn B in appearance, with an angled roof and twin curved windscreens, albeit surmounted by a tower with chevrons on each side. However, the equipment of Brush 'Chopper' controls would now be mounted in the saloon, under the luggage racks by the doors. Clearly, it had been decided to avoid the problems which had previously been created by the roof-mounted Vambac equipment on the Coronations, which had been affected by blowing sand. The livery would be in cream and two shades of green, keeping to the current fleet style of upper-green and lower-cream, albeit relieved by a zig-zag green line along the side and round the front. By October, present in the Works was a complete pair of bogies, 'Chopper' control had been delivered, and the body for 641 was expected towards the end of January 1984. By February that year I was told that the body of 641 was nearly complete at East Lancs Coachbuilders, and it looked very long with rubber fenders at each end and recessed lights. Ironically, Brush car 638 – the prototype OMO trial car – which had been out of use since 1980, was now scrapped in the yard at Rigby Road. Suffice to say that it needed to make way for the new tram and the visiting trams led by Edinburgh 35 for the Centenary in the following year.

The arrival of 641 took place on 17th April 1984, when it made its journey on a low-loader from East Lancs factory in Blackburn. Being lunchtime, there was quite a gathering of workmen who gave a cheer to celebrate its departure, and police escorts accompanied 641 on the low-loader along Whalley New Road. This was my first sight of the new tram, and certainly it looked long, but its somewhat flat roof was surmounted by large advertising boxes. These displayed an appropriate message for the occasion:- on the front 'EAST LANCS COACHBUILDERS ARE PROUD OF THEIR CONTRIBUTION TO 100 YEARS OF TRANSPORT' – and side – '1885 – 1985 BRITAIN'S FIRST ELECTRIC TRAMWAY CELEBRATES IT'S *(sic)* CENTENARY'. The Municipal coat-of-arms was on the panel next to the front door, and a miniature crest was in the centre of the front, just below the windscreen. The livery was exactly as shown on the plan, but the pantograph tower was not fitted for the journey. So that there would be no doubt as to its destination 641 naturally showed 'TOWER' on its slim indicator screen.

I followed its steady journey via Samlesbury to the Whitbread Brewery where 641's body was weighed as 9.55 tonnes, which together with the bogies equalled 17.29 tonnes in unladen weight. By 2.30pm the low-loader left for the M6, making the unusual sight of a new tram proceeding along the motorway. Once in Blackpool the entourage proceeded down Squires Gate Lane and turned into Lytham Road, along this well-known former Squires Gate tram route, and passengers at the bus stops stared at it with surprise. Finally, 641 arrived at Rigby Road depot and the low-loader reversed inside, following the white-painted lines

During 641's trial run on 8th June 1984 at the Cliffs, passing OMO 5 offers a marked contrast in style, colours, and livery application. *(Author)*

parallel with track 17 leading to the electrical compound. The new arrival was soon in position, and four jacks were in place to take the weight so that the low-loader could withdraw. The bogies were rolled into place and the lowering of the body commenced; however, the engineers noticed that the rubbing-plates had been wrongly positioned, and so 641 had to be left elevated on the jacks until the following day. Since this was after normal hours, the East Lancs staff arrived on the following morning to alter them. General comments about the new tram were favourable by the local staff, but I did ask one of the East Lancs officials there as to why the roof looked somewhat low and flat, and the reply was that the drawings could be adapted for a double-deck tram, using the same design. So there is an answer to my question, although we have never seen any East Lancs double-deckers yet.

During the afternoon of 6th June 641 was cautiously taken out of the depot and made its first run on the Promenade. At the curve into Lytham Road, the engineers watched the bogies and the lifeguards and noticed that the latter seemed low and indeed caught on the road surface. Pursued by a tower-wagon along the Promenade, clearly 641 showed good acceleration and left it behind. Number 641's trial run round the system started at 4am on 8th June, by journeying to Fleetwood. It returned to depot by 7.50am for the engineers' breakfast, and then travelled to Tower, Pleasure Beach and Little Bispham, returning to the depot by the end of the morning. On 15th June, 641 was taken to Talbot Square for a formal ceremony by Councillor Stanley Parkinson, and he named it 'The Centenary Belle' though this was subsequently abbreviated. The Railway Inspector examined it on 29th June and passed it for service. Drivers were then trained on 641 and it entered Fleetwood service on Friday 6th July. This was the first appearance of a completely new tram in service since the Coronations in 1952. However, surprising news came that there was to be a second car of the same type on trial, but equipped differently by General Electric Company. The same type of East Lancs body was to be mounted on a pair of ex-Coronation Maley & Taunton bogies, obtained from Beamish and rebuilt by Wickhams. The new car was numbered 651. In order to compare the new 641 with remaining Coronation 660 Fylde Tramway Society had a tour with both cars on Sunday 21st June. I remember travelling on them to compare their riding qualities and found that 641 rode smoothly and did not bounce like 660. However, I felt that Coronation 660 had a better saloon with its spacious and glazed interior, giving ideal passenger environment qualities. In reality the Coronations had been phased out and therefore 641 started the new generation of trams for Blackpool.

Promenade Tramway Centenary 1985

Undoubtedly, 641 arrived in a year of fascinating moves by trams of all types, with regard to the Centenary of the tramway in the following year. Also of significant importance was the completion of track relaying in Lord Street, Fleetwood with the road surface relaid in February 1984. Edinburgh 35 – which had arrived in November 1983 – was repainted in the traditional livery of maroon and white with gold lining and numerals. On 21st April, its Lothian Transport owners were taken for a ride along the Promenade, after which it went into service from 4.30pm and carried its first passengers since 1956. On Monday 2nd April, Balloon 710 left for the National Tramway Museum at Crich, in exchange for Glasgow Cunarder 1297 which arrived on 5th April. The Scottish tram was first fitted with a pantograph and went on trials the next day to Fleetwood, where it missed the overhead on the curves of the Ferry loop line and had to be towed back. Subsequently fitted with a trolley, it successfully journeyed to Fleetwood on 24th April, making a fine sight and reminding passers-by of its Glasgow days. On 11th April Miss Blackpool launched Blackpool Standard 40 at Crich, ready for its return for the Centenary. On the following day in Blackpool, The Great Tram Race was held on the Promenade between Edinburgh 35 and Glasgow 1297, and surprisingly 35 won. Next, engineering car 754 left Blackpool on 17th July for restoration as Marton Box car 31 at Beamish, in exchange for their Sheffield

Top: Another contrast – this time between Coronation 660 and newly-returned (from Crich) Standard 40 seen at Pleasure Beach loop on 6th May 1985. The Roberts' cars design has stood the test of time well; a fleet of these (with modern chopper control?) would not look out-of-place on the Promenade today. *(Author)*

Balloon 710 at Crich Town End, with Cliff Quarry in the background. Standard 49 and Prague 189 are following number 710 which has been exchanged as part of the celebration and as seen left. The Museum currently has eight former Blackpool cars in its collection, though not all are on public display. *(Author)*

An historic sight as Conduit car 4 poses at North Pier on 13th July 1985 for its handover ceremony. It was running on batteries by then. *(Tony Stevenson)*

GEC 651 at Gynn Square on a trial run, looking much the same as 641, apart from the M & T bogies. *(Terry Daniel)*

Roberts car 513. This came on 24th October and made its first passenger journey in Blackpool for the Fylde Tramway Society Christmas tour on 26th December. I always remember one of the Beamish staff coming downstairs on to the driver's platform at Fleetwood and warning us that the speed was too great on the sleeper track. Certainly, this 4-wheeler moved with a rocking motion, and many years later in April 2003 513 disgraced itself by derailing.

The events of the Centenary Year 1985 were memorable, starting with the departure of the first Boat, 603, for San Francisco, USA, having previously been in Philadelphia for the Bi-Centenary in 1976. On Monday 27th March GEC 651 appeared, looking like 641, but with different bogies under the body. On that same day Boat 607 left on loan to NTM at Crich, in exchange for Standard 40 which arrived a few days later. At the beginning of May, Boat 600 departed for Heaton Park in exchange for their unique Manchester California car 765, which would enhance the Centenary Year in Blackpool. The Fylde Tramway Society was provided with an interesting collection of trams during its tours for its annual Convention weekend in May! Naturally, it started with open-top Balloon 706, its upper-deck panels being decorated by 'FTS Congratulates Blackpool Transport for their Tramway Centenary'. While the novelty of riding on such a recreated 1934 open-topper was a first time event for most enthusiasts, there were a few who remembered riding them in the 'thirties. While 706 looked fine, it differed from its original appearance by being fitted with upper-deck front windscreens and a mini-roof carrying a pantograph. This spoilt its appearance, but eventually, when passengers complained about the grease used to lubricate the overhead wire dropping down onto their clothes and staining them, the trolley was restored and made it look more authentic. Also during the weekend, enthusiasts enjoyed a tour on Dreadnought 59 and Standard 40 which were both in the same pre-1933 red-and-white livery, followed on Monday by two Roberts-built trams, Coronation 660 and Sheffield 513. Next to arrive were Manchester California 765 and Blackpool Pantograph car 167, which were handed over at the depot on Saturday 11th May by representatives from the Manchester society and the Tramcar Sponsorship Organisation, following which they had an excursion to Fleetwood. During the journey, heads were turned

Two number tens, but two very different trams – OMO 10 and Howth 10 – on the day before the Centenary events on a tour at Harrowside by the open-topper. Work carried out during the regauging and recommissioning of the Irish veteran cured the derailing problems which had plagued the car on its own system, and the spell in Blackpool has therefore been the most successful – and satisfying – period in its long life. *(Author)*

by the public as they saw a red Manchester tram here for the first time, though many remembered Pantograph car 167, which was familiar on the Fleetwood route until 1961.

Official Centenary events were launched by the well-known comedian Les Dawson, who started a parade of trams at North Pier. He was also filmed travelling on Dreadnought 59, amusingly reminiscent about his experiences on Blackpool trams. A Royal event on 6th June featured Princess Alice, who travelled on Standard 40 from Starr Gate to North Pier, where she unveiled the plaque on 706, fittingly named after herself. The Open Day at the depot and works on 16th June provided an opportunity for the public to visit and have tours round the workshops. There was a shuttle service from the Tower, using some of the visiting trams from Sheffield, Glasgow and Edinburgh.

Clearly, the most historic tram of the Centenary was Conduit car 4 of 1885, which was restored under the direction of Derek Shepherd at the Museum of Science & Industry in Manchester, restoring the original truck and chain-driven motor. To restore it to 1885 appearance, the trolley was removed and batteries fitted under the saloon's longitudinal seats so that it appeared to move like a conduit car. It was formally handed over to Blackpool at North Pier on 13th July and subsequently driven along Princess Street in its 1885 setting. However, on Sunday 14th July, the Fleetwood Transport Festival was held for the first time, with a rally of historic road vehicles displayed along the closed main streets, together with a splendid tram service, ideal for viewing, between Ash Street and the Ferry. Of course, it became known as 'Tram Sunday', unique in being able to offer rides on trams from six different systems, together with open-top historic Blackpool Dreadnought 59 and 706.

The final tram to arrive for the Centenary was open-top Hill of Howth 10, re-gauged from 5ft 3in, which it used in Ireland, and displayed on the new siding at North Pier. Here it was welcomed by actress Joanna Lumley, who also switched on the Illuminations that night. The climax of the Centenary Day arrived on Sunday 29th September, and on the day before there was a fascinating Promenade service with trams in a variety of colours from other systems. Celebrating the original inaugural procession in 1885, one hundred years later the procession from North Pier to the Pleasure Beach comprised 20 trams led by Conduit car 4, carrying guests in historic costumes. Thousands lined the route to watch the fascinating parade of Blackpool trams, together with guest trams of all shapes and sizes. The climax was achieved by 1885 steam tram-engine 'John Bull' which was built by Beyer, Peacock of Manchester in 1885, exported to New South Wales, Australia, then retrieved by its manufacturer in 1890 and subsequently used as a works shunter. This was without doubt the finest tramway occasion in the Twentieth Century, celebrated on a fine and sunny day. More light hearted events involved competitive teams pulling Sheffield 513 by rope in Princess Street. The Last Night on the Prom provided a finale on Sunday 27th October, with a procession to Pleasure Beach

(Above) Crowds on Lytham Road watching Conduit 4 and Dreadnought 59 leaving for the procession from North Pier to the Pleasure Beach on 29th September 1985. It is perhaps hard to imagine more different cars than these two, both representing the late 1800s and both now unique.

(Below) A wonderful scene of the Tower, below left, with the procession, showing Howth 10 and Manchester 765, whilst right we see cars arriving at Pleasure Beach, with 607, Glasgow 1297, OMO 8 and Sheffield 513 in a glorious melange. *(All Author)*

Centenary 641 is seen on service for Starr Gate, waiting at the
Manchester Square stop, followed by a Balloon. *(Author)*

loop, where a buffet was served on Coronation 660, followed by a firework display at North Pier. The historic
trams then returned to depot – I travelled on 1297 at speed – successfully concluding that memorable year!

Following the fascinating activities of the Centenary Year, 1986 saw the end of Blackpool Corporation
Transport Department, when Blackpool Transport Services Ltd (BTS) came into being on 20th October and
took over operation on Sunday 26th. By then most trams and buses had the Municipal coat-of-arms replaced
by a logo showing 'BLACKPOOL TRANSPORT' with the Tower and sea-waves.

At this time three new Centenary cars 642–4 had been completed at East Lancs, but were waiting for the
controllers and equipment from the Brush Company. They would be delivered in November, and three new
sets of bogies were waiting in the depot. A further three Centenary cars 645–7 were on order for delivery by
April and were to be financed by Blackpool Borough Council shares in BTS.

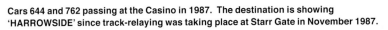

Cars 644 and 762 passing at the Casino in 1987. The destination is showing
'HARROWSIDE' since track-relaying was taking place at Starr Gate in November 1987.

Centenary 644 having reversed, passengers are waiting for a return journey to Fleetwood, while Starr Gate loop is being relaid. A blank indicator is unusual. *(Author)*

Managing Director Tony Depledge (who had followed Derek Hyde in charge) told me that 651 was to be equipped with the same bogies and equipment as the other Centenaries, which would make eight such cars, and, together with the two Jubilee cars, would make ten OPO cars (as they were now known) to cover the winter service. It then looked as though Centenaries 648–50 were unlikely to materialise. The seating layout of the new Centenary cars would follow the style of 651, and advertising boxes like 641 were to be built and fitted at Blackpool – but were not. Subsequently, it is clear that further Centenary cars were never ordered but it seems that a further two should have completed the required ten cars. In reality, today the Jubilee cars are seen on the winter service looking somewhat empty, but operated as OPOs for economy.

Later that year, track renewal north of Pleasure Beach meant that the winter service was terminating at Manchester Square, with a bus shuttle service to Starr Gate. The service was operated by OMOs with Centenary 641, but 643 was delivered on 11th November and was soon in the workshop being fitted with the pantograph tower. By Christmas the three Centenary cars had arrived and they would enter service in January 1987, when the Brush Company had commissioned them on 6th January. This allowed OMO 3 to be replaced by 643 then 6 and 7 by 644 and 642. New track had been completed to Dean Street crossover by Christmas and a new crossover had been installed at Pleasure Beach to enable cars to reverse there when the loop-line was closed for the winter. Incidentally, during extremely cold weather in January 1987, it was found that brakes on 641, 761 and 762 were frozen on for a week in the depot. When 643 entered service on 24th February, OMO 3 was dragged on to the parking yard for scrapping, where 2 had already been. Of the remaining OMOs, 1, 5, 8, and 11 were in the green livery and 6, 7, 9 and 12 were in red, while 10 was advertising Bispham Kitchens in yellow. However, a new career was planned for OMO 7, which was withdrawn in February and left for Salford Mode Wheel on 16th March, to be rebuilt as a replica Tramroad Vanguard car. Centenaries 642 and 644 entered service in February 1987, and OMO 6 was repanelled and repainted in April. Vanguard 619 arrived on Wednesday 29th July, looking correct apart from a tower with pantograph on the roof. The Railway Inspector saw it on 31st July and said that it needed to have full-width lifeguards and more powerful lights. Work continued on making wooden reversible seats at Salford, which were delivered in August. Unfortunately, the Inspector failed 619 once again, condemning the four platform lattice gates and requiring an undertaking that they would be dealt with, before it was operated. The off side entrance gates had been fixed when it operated on 27th September, and 619 was found to be ideal for viewing the Illuminations. Centenary 645 operated in the same month, and Brush had fitted the electrical equipment at Blackpool along with 646, which appeared sparkling new in service on 4th December. The

final conventional Centenary car 647 went into service on 30th April 1988 completing the scheduled class, apart from the later acquisition of 651 which would be re-equipped and renumbered as 648.

In 1988 the Centenary cars were all in service, and seven of them looked better without the advertising boxes on the roof. However, movement of trams continued when Boat 606, painted in royal blue and yellow, left in March for Glasgow Garden Festival, together with Edinburgh 35. They were joined there by Paisley 68, Glasgow 22 and 1297, all from the National Tramway Museum. Next, on 14th June, 1914 - built saloon car, Box 40, arrived from Heaton Park having been rewired, repanelled, retyred and repainted there, ready for the 90th anniversary of the Blackpool & Fleetwood Tramroad in 1988. After making a preliminary trip to North Pier, one motor failed and had to be rewound and returned in July, ready for its first tour to Fleetwood since 1963. By this time the correct facia boards had been fitted above the saloon windows, but unfortunately advertising ones were mounted between the bogies. To complete its appearance, 40's seats were subsequently removed for re-upholstering in moquette with a ruby tartan pattern, formerly used in Blackpool Transport's Swift buses.

Tram Sunday that year featured Box 40, making its first appearance at the head of the procession, followed by Howth 10, Bolton 66, Dreadnought 59, Boat 607 and Princess Alice 706. In the same year, Brush car 636 was repainted in the wartime Railcoach livery and a tour was held on 17th August with Philip Higgs driving it, and wearing a wartime tin hat and carrying a gas mask! On 21st October open-top Hill of Howth 10 toured the system on its final tour, patronised by Clifton Flewitt, a famous native of Dublin. The final Centenary 648 was next ready for service, with Brush equipment fitted, and its first full day of operation was 5th January 1990. At the same time 641 was lifted in the Body Shop to have its body overhauled and its wheels re-tyred. Incidentally, it was found that its window frames were rusted and had to be replaced after only six years in service. So this had been the first decade for the Centenary cars, replacing the OMOs, and now the livery was re-styled in cream, with green roof and skirt round the lower panels. A few of the OMOs survived, including 5 repainted in the new livery in 1992 and whilst this was flattering to the OMO body style, it remained unique.

With the introduction of the eight Centenary cars, and two Jubilee cars, it would have been expected that OMOs would completely be phased out. However owing to trouble at first with the cam switches and auxiliary contacts, several continued until 1993. OMOs 5, 8 and 11 were used in January 1992 after several Centenary cars developed alternator faults, also two were immobilised at Rossall because of frost on the

(Upper) On Tram Sunday 1988, Box 40 has returned and is seen next to Bolton 66 at the Ferry. Note the former has not yet been fitted with the municipal indicator box.

(Centre) Crossbench car 619, rebuilt from OMO 7, seen on Lord Street on Tram Sunday 1991 later in the afternoon.

(Lower) Brush car 636 in a Railcoach-style wartime livery, seen at Casino in 1989. Originally it had cream flares on the sides and slimmer separate Vs at each end. *(Author all)*

The End Draws Near For The OMO Cars

(Top) OMO cars 3 and 10 on the promenade on a dull day showing two methods of current collection, traditional pole and single arm pantograph. *(James Millington)*

(Centre) OMO 5 in its final version of the new livery seen at Cleveleys at Christmas 1992 shows a third method of current collection. *(James Millington)*

(Below) OMO 8, having been repainted in the 'plum and custard' livery in October 2005, in the Body Shop with 648. *(Author)*

Refurbishment Of The Centenary Cars

(Above) Tram Sunday 2006, and 642 is seen in plain yellow, showing the shaped indicator and original windscreens. *(Robert Fergusson)*

(Centre) Number 646 at Norbreck in 2006, showing the revised appearance of four of the Centenary cars. *(Bryan Grint)*

(Below) Number 645 seen in the Body Shop in October 2005, with the low-fronted skirts and flat windscreen. Alongside, 717 is being rebuilt. *(Author)*

overhead line. Buses took over the service from Thornton Gate to Fleetwood, and since 647's brakes failed at The Metropole, buses operated the whole tram route for several days. By February, four OMOs were in use, including No. 10 advertising Bispham Kitchens which was about to be replaced in this role by Centenary 644. In May OMO 5 returned to service once work had taken place on the body frame, but in the same month 8 was withdrawn from traffic being in poor condition and having last been repainted in 1985. By June, 5 and 11 were still in use on the Fleetwood route almost every day, but by July they were only used as specials with conductors. Other interesting changes involved the Boats being fitted with the EE Z-6 controllers, while 602 and 604 were fitted with pantographs and used on Tram Sunday. Passengers then found that their clothing was being stained, resulting from pantograph friction with the overhead and so the trolleys were restored and Boats returned to their traditional appearance. By the final month in the year, OMO 11 replaced 762 during the day because of a shortfall in the number of Centenaries available, but 5 was suffering from faults on the inverter, which restricted it to daylight operations. By this time, parts were being removed from 8, it having last operated in May 1992. This situation clearly indicated that there should have been ten Centenary cars, in order to provide spares for those operating.

The finale for the OMOs took place early in 1993. Whilst 641 was being repainted in the new style, following its refitting with new window frames, 5 and 11 were in frequent use during January. By March, however, OMO 5 and 11 were confined to depot, but on Thursday 11th March, 11 replaced 647 and later in the day was itself replaced by Centenary car 644 at Manchester Square, after a final decision was made by Engineering and Traffic Departments.

In their second decade, the Centenary cars were the mainstay of the Blackpool and Fleetwood route for half of the year, have been rebuilt to change their original appearance. The first was 642 in 1998, which appeared in May 1999 with a higher indicator box and display panels over the windows, which made it look better proportioned than it had originally. The new window frames had opening top sections on each and black surrounds, while the seats in the saloon were re-covered with a good pattern of moquette. Originally, 642 was painted in yellow, being the first Centenary not in the fleet livery. In August 2000, 641 was the second Centenary car to be redesigned, following the same appearance as 642 with a new pantograph tower, thus removing the advertisement boxes and its original tower. It went into Kit-Kat livery of red-and-white, unfortunately covering the windows for the first time, unlike cars in Amsterdam with the same Kit-Kat adverts.

Subsequently, each of the Centenaries has been refurbished, with new panelling, window frames, doors and flat windscreens, together with higher roof sides and matching indicators. Thus, they look different from 642 and 641 and yet further changes came with 645 in 2005, having bonded glazed twin windscreens, a low frontage replacing the lifeguards and curved corners at each end. Number 648, being the only Centenary retaining the original appearance, remained in service in 2005. However, it has now been partially refurbished, keeping its front appearance with slim indicators, curved windscreen and headlamps in black mask. While the sides and windows are altered, the roof panels taper down below the original indicators, thus facilitating it being returned to its original appearance, if ultimately preserved. Although the Centenary cars have provided Blackpool with modern trams during the past 20 years, their future will depend upon the outcome of the requirement for trams to have easy-access for the disabled. However, if articulated cars – Skoda Astra or Tram Power – are introduced to the Starr Gate and Fleetwood service, Centenaries should still survive as Promenade-specials, having been a successful generation of trams in the post-war fleet.

In July OMO 11 was sent to Carnforth, where it was fitted with a new bogie for trial under an articulated car belonging to Tram Power in Blackpool.

Tram Power wished to demonstrate that it is possible to build a modern low floor vehicle which can compete with the Continental models, at much lower cost, and in so doing provide a boost for the British economy rather than, as at present, relying on imported trams.

The arrival of the new Roadliner articulated tram was, therefore, very significant. Built in Britain it is designed for use on new or existing light-rail schemes such as are found in Manchester, Sheffield, Birmingham, Croydon, Nottingham and Dublin. Numbered 611, it was first seen on 2nd June at 5 o' clock in the morning, travelling to Fleetwood with the Railway Inspector on board. Unfortunately, it was not passed for use and, therefore, was not seen subsequently, apart from its demonstration on the depot open day. It left for Cardiff in August 2000 for modifications, was then used for trials at Birkenhead on the Wirral Heritage Tramway where it was able to be run on extended test on the private tracks.

After scrutiny and approval by the Railway Inspector, it came to Blackpool on 7th December 2005 for a further trial, by then in the striking 14 bus route livery. Its length is 29 metres, weight is 22 tons and by now it had new smaller and more powerful motors, and an inverter. Professor Lewis Lesley of Tram Power Ltd. has commented that 611 will be able to operate at higher speeds, and to compete with buses on operating costs, speed and comfort, carrying up to 200 passengers, including 85 seated. Daily trials continued in Blackpool until it caught fire on 24th January 2007 at Manchester Square when returning to the depot. It is expected that one section of 611 will be rebuilt for possible future use in Blackpool.

Number 611 was on display at Fleetwood Ferry with Coronation 660 on Tram Sunday 16th July 2006, and was subsequently caught on camera whilst returning to Rigby Road. Sadly, it was very badly damaged by an electrical fire on 24th January 2007 at Manchester Square, shortly before completing a satisfactory period of non-revenue operation.
(Robert Fergusson)

A cheerful group of dedicated enthusiasts on Dreadnought 59 on a frosty 13th January, 1963, with Keith Terry posing as driver, Bob Parr (extreme left) photographing the Vambac behind, and David Tudor leaning over the top rails for the photographer. (Dennis Gill)

Tram Tours And Their Fans 1939 – 2006

Imagine a quiet Sunday afternoon in the high street of a northern town with the shining steel track of the tramway down the centre, and local people looking in the shop windows. Suddenly, round the corner comes an very unusual tram – the open-top Dreadnought 59. The pedestrians are astonished when it halts and disgorges many men of varied ages, who take lots of photographs to record this event. Passers-by either smile knowingly, or shake their heads in disbelief, for this is not a publicity stunt but merely a tram enthusiasts' tour. The town is Fleetwood, where the one remaining main street in Britain still has its original tram route with a wide variety of trams, hence its survival. Fifty years ago, similar scenes could have been seen in Glasgow, Liverpool, Leeds, Sheffield, Edinburgh, Aberdeen or Dundee, where tram fans from all parts of the country shared experiences in travelling on a tram tour to all parts of the system – though not in Dreadnoughts, they were exclusive to Blackpool. Modern light rail systems can be found today in Manchester, Sheffield, Croydon and Birmingham, but Blackpool is the only place with its original tramway. Only if you have been on a tour can you recapture the pleasure of sharing experiences with fellow enthusiasts who savour every moment, including taking the tram on little-used track. Occasionally, the inevitable happens, and the tram may respond to unusual locations by jumping the track and halting in the tarmac of the road.

Each situation is recorded for posterity by keen photographers, creating evidence for future historians to study and identify the causes. I hope you find this chapter interesting and amusing but spare a thought for those who have to put the trams back on the lines . . .

The whole idea of holding tram tours for enthusiasts began in 1938, when the newly-formed Light Railway Transport League organised an epic 30 mile journey across London, from Waltham Cross in the north to Purley in the south, to publicise the modernising of the tramway for the future. However, this soon changed, as the columns of *Modern Tramway* revealed, with tours in Birmingham, Liverpool, Leicester, Southend and many others being held where the future was questionable. On 11th June 1939, the League arrived in Blackpool to sample the new streamlined trams which had recently entered service. Blackpool Borough Transport was under the energetic managership of Walter Luff, who later became League President. Under the 'Five Year Plan' he had modernised the tramway fleet by replacing old trams with an entirely new fleet of 116 streamliners of several different types. Under the title 'A Tale of Three Trams' the Modern Tramway reporter recorded for posterity the events of that pioneer tour in Blackpool. "The first chosen car was Boat 235, a modern open toastrack which was waiting on the siding in Talbot Square". Modest posters proclaiming that this was an LRTL tour were fixed on the fenders and hung from the trolley-tower. After the journey along the Promenade, 235 ventured on to the street track in Squires Gate Lane and passed the Lytham St Annes depot, by this time a bus garage: "Catching a glimpse of the last remaining Lytham St Annes car 41 in the depot". This was the Pullman car which had been retained when the rest of the fleet had been broken up in 1937, but was subsequently sacrificed in 1941 towards the war effort. Today enthusiasts would not have missed a golden opportunity for a scoop picture and to raise a fund for its preservation! The second part of the tour was by double-decker 258, and then for a ride to Fleetwood on Railcoach 274. "The amenities included an interior saloon clock, and this was carefully corrected before the start. In the Norbreck neighbourhood some fast running was enjoyed and LRTL founder Mr JW Fowler entered the motorman's cab to add some footage to the League's film library. On the return journey from Fleetwood a halt was made at Bispham where 274 travelled down Red Bank Road for a visit to the depot. This was full of trams of older types including toastracks, non-streamlined single-deck saloons and crossbench cars. There was also an interesting old works car numbered 4 – of 1885 origin – and the electric loco which was used to haul railway wagons to Thornton Gate sidings. So 274 returned to Blundell Street after a very memorable day." This contemporary account of the first tour in Blackpool established a pattern repeated many times in the future, and is fascinating to read 68 years later.

In post-war years, the attention of the LRTL became dominated by those tramways which were threatened with closure, but on 26th October 1947 they had a Blackpool tour on newly-equipped car 208. In 1949, just before the Southampton system closed down on 31st December, the LRTL enjoyed a tour on open-top car 64. Some of the group subsequently purchased 45, it being in better condition, for the princely sum of £10. This

Railcoach 274 at Fleetwood Ferry with an LRTL group posing at its door, prior to its departure for Bispham. Note the promotional posters in the windows, and on the front fender. Today this Railcoach is Twin-car 674 and 209 (behind) is the Western Train. *(WA Camwell – NTM Col.)*

New TMS members on board Southampton 45 outside Marton depot, it having been handed over to their Chairman Major Walker by LRTL Chairman JW Fowler in 1955. *(Dennis Gill)*

was the first example of amateur preservation, and since no tramway museum existed for storage, friendly undertakings were approached to help them with 45's storage. The car first went to Leeds, but spent most of its retirement in Blackpool's Marton depot by courtesy of Walter Luff.

A Museum Committee of the LRTL was formed to respond to the increasing demand to preserve items from the tramway age, which by the early 'fifties was under threat of vanishing completely. Southampton 45 was the first success story, since it survived into the age of the Tramway Museum Society which was formed in 1955. The League Convention in Blackpool of July 1955 formed the setting for a unique ceremony at Marton depot, where 45 was driven out by Mr JW Fowler of the League, parked on the siding outside the depot, and the controller-key was handed over to Major CSN Walker of the new Tramway Museum Society. The car, under its new ownership, was driven back inside by Major Walker, and thus the tramway museum movement was founded. Southampton 45 gathered dust at the back of Marton Depot for a further two years, behind a row of Standards on the east side of the depot. Rather a shame that no tour was allowed on 45 in Blackpool! It then went to the Montagu Motor Museum at Beaulieu in Hampshire for display, along with Newcastle 102. Eventually, they arrived at the new Crich Tramway Museum site – 45 in 1960 then 102 in 1975 – and are there to this day.

However, the main story of tours at Blackpool is prefaced by the intention of Walter Luff, before his retirement in 1954, to break up all the Standards and relegate the Balloons to seasonal use only. The 25 Coronations which were delivered 1952-4, were bought to complete the single-deck fleet. This never came to fruition, and under new Manager JC Franklin the Standards got a new lease of life. They had been used as 'Prom-specials' in 1953/4, when rainy weather precluded any of the dozen Boat-cars operating from Marton depot. However, in Autumn 1956, the introduction of Illumination Tours by tram used the traditional Standards with a high seating capacity of 78 and suitable for good all-round viewing. Each weekend the enclosed Standards would leave Marton depot at 6pm and travel to Central Station via Royal Oak and Lytham Road. Here they coped with the huge queue which often stretched from Woolworths past the Tower towards Victoria Street stop. The survival of the Standards prepared the way for many enjoyable tram tours on a traditional British double-decker, until their final demise in 1966. It was in 1957 that Keith Terry of

Leeds – a name long associated with organising tours at Blackpool – persuaded the Transport Department to hire balcony Standard 40 for a tour. At first they denied its existence, since only eight totally-enclosed Standards – 41, 48, 49, 143, 147, 158, 159, and 160 – were licensed for service. However, there were a further seven Standard cars at Marton depot, including five balcony cars 28, 40, 145, 152, 153 and enclosed cars 42 and 177. These had survived the holocaust at Blundell Street depot, and when it became a bus garage in 1954 they were moved back to Marton depot. Another balcony car, 144, still existed, in the Seashore Museum, U.S.A., having left Blackpool in 1955 and been shipped from Liverpool to Boston. These remaining seven Standards were progressively stripped of their fittings, but fortunately 40 still remained intact. After Keith's requests, Blackpool Transport allowed 40 to be used for a tour on 7th April 1957, and sent Traffic Superintendent Bill Etough along to supervise it. With a fine spirit of adventure 40 crossed the carriageway at Foxhall and made a rare journey down Princess Street before the amazed residents and it returned to the main depot a different way. The occasion must have made such an impression on Bill Etough that no enthusiasts tour was allowed to follow that same route until 1978 when under new management. When the six stripped Standards were taken to Thornton Gate for scrapping in April 1958, Balcony 40 stayed at Marton depot and was licensed for use in the seasons which followed. Of course, in January 1963 it was presented to the National Tramway Museum, runs there to this day and did make one visit to Blackpool in 1985 for the Centenary of the Promenade Tramway.

Following Keith's success in saving 40 during the previous year, he hired it once again in 1958, when it was accompanied by a repainted 41, hired by Keith Pearson to follow 40 wherever it ventured. This provided more seats for keen enthusiasts who could not ride on 40 and yet took part in a memorable event. Being Standards of two types they made a fine pair, first posing at Station Road terminus with South Pier behind them. They then travelled north to Thornton Gate, where they were passed by twin car 276-275 coming from Fleetwood on the new Coastal Tour. Cars 40 and 41 then travelled along Dickson Road to North Station – a sight which I had not previously seen – and finally along Squires Gate Lane, used only by Boats on the Circular Tour. In the following year, there was a May weekend with three tours on trams of different types. It began with green Balloon 244 in handsome traditional livery, which journeyed round the street routes. Returning from Squires Gate, at Royal Oak the point-boy turned points into Waterloo Road but 244 lost its trolley because he did not remember to pull the frog. So the crew retrieved it, and 244 was able to proceed to

A photographic extravaganza for one and all – including the Author – admiring and photographing Standard 40 at Rossall siding, the balcony car having made its first journey to Fleetwood on 24th May 1959. *(Dennis Gill)*

A fascinating scene as Twin-car 276-275 on the Coastal Tour passes the historic Standards 40 and
41 at Thornton Gate, while reversing on their tour. Local boys observe it too! *(Dennis Gill)*

Marton depot. On the following morning at 8am. I boarded Balcony 40 at Central Station before it proceeded
to South Promenade to collect the large tour party. This was its first visit to Fleetwood since the check-rail
fitted to the track made it possible. Being a sunny morning it was possible for us to have a photo-stop for 40
in a deserted Lord Street on the corner of London Street. At the Ferry Standard 40 could be pictured with
service Coronations and Brush cars, and then with the Pharos lighthouse. A visit to Bispham depot enabled
us to have Engineering car 3 brought out into the yard and pictured with 40, while visitors satisfied their
curiosity by going inside the depot. In the afternoon a tour by Pantographs 169 and 175 saw them in unusual
locations, since they were normally only seen on the North Station and Fleetwood service. Thus their trolleys
were fitted with the swivel heads and travelled on the route from South Pier to Marton depot. Since the
doors were open the two Pantograph cars were driven inside, making them an unusual sight amongst the
Marton Vambacs there. Finally, they followed the Circular Tour route along Squires Gate Lane and returned
to the Rigby Road depot via Lytham Road. This weekend surely featured as a momentous occasion for tours
in Blackpool, but in wildest imagination one could not expect anything to surpass it, and yet the 75th
Anniversary was to follow in 1960!

(Upper) Conduit 1 stopped near the Derby Baths for passengers to change, during the TMS tour on 9th July 1960. *(Author)*

(Lower) The final ride on Dreadnought 59 in February 1965 at Rossall Beach, where something has certainly attracted the attention of upper-deck passengers. *(Author)*

During that winter the Transport Department was busy restoring four of the old fleet cars for the 75th Anniversary on 29 September 1960. Former Conduit car 4 was driven from Bispham depot to the Works, followed by Crossbench car 2 from Copse Road depot and Dreadnought 59 towed from the same location. Saloon Box 40 showed "ENGINEERING CAR" on its indicator, but was only driven a short way from Rigby Road depot into the Body Shop. By the time that the annual Terry Tours took place on 22nd May, only Crossbench 2 was ready and so posed outside the depot with Standard 160 and Twin-car 276-275. The following tour on 160 was remarkable mainly for being driven at fast speed and so pitched and rolled along Lytham Road track, confirming its bad state. By this time the National Tramway Museum had been established at Crich, and its Newsletter, with a map of how to reach it, were being distributed. The most memorable tour of that year took place on Saturday 9th July, when the vintage trams 1, 2 and 59 went into passenger service, and were hired by the Tramway Museum Society for a ride to Fleetwood. When the crowd of enthusiasts arrived at the depot they saw only the diminutive 1885 car 1 there and Crossbench 2 and

(Upper) A contrasting scene with Box 40 at South Pier during its March 1961 tour, along with Burlingham bus No. 204. *(John Fozard)*

(Lower) Conduit 1 passing the Coliseum Coach Station on its Sunday morning shuttle tour of Lytham Road in March 1961. Notice a full saloon and empty top-deck, following the rules of engagement dutifully. *(John Fozard)*

Dreadnought 59 were out on the Promenade. Urgent phone calls had to be made for Inspectors to send them back to the depot. While we waited for them, the opportunity was taken to explore the depot, which at the time contained restored B & F Box 40 and new Maley & Taunton bogies waiting for trailers. Eventually, the tour procession commenced with Conduit 1 leading, followed by 2 and 59. At Starr Gate we had a chance to capture these three historic cars together and a group photograph was taken. On a perfect day the riding to Fleetwood undoubtedly provided our first experiences of ride upon the Dreadnought open-top deck and also on crossbench seats of the Blackpool & Fleetwood car. At Bispham 1885 car 1 had to be left there and its passengers crowded on the other two trams for the ride to Fleetwood. I travelled on 2 capturing the days of the Tramroad and returned on 59, enjoying the top-deck ride in the sunshine. Pictures were taken in Pharos Street with the lighthouse and everyone who took part in that trip will recall it as a highlight of the many tram tours in Blackpool. The vintage cameo was enhanced by the news that the first of the new trailers was to leave the MCW factory for Blackpool on the following day. Certainly the future seemed promising!

By 1961 the impending closure of the Squires Gate route influenced all tour planning in the organisers' desire to cover all sections of the track which would be abandoned. The Blackpool & Fylde Tramway Historical Association (BFTHA, later Fylde Tramway Society, FTS) became involved in tour organisation, and on 25th and 26th March I held tours with novel features. Box car 40 first proceeded to Fleetwood and used crossovers in North Albert Street and Broadwater, and then visited Rossall siding and Bispham depot. Later in the tour, the car disgraced itself when it derailed on Bloomfield Road crossover in Lytham Road, right outside the shop of the Chairman of the Transport Committee. Fortunately, the car was driven back on to the rails, and made off for South Pier, then Squires Gate Lane and reversed at St Annes Road crossover on the Marton route. On the following morning the little 1885 car made three short tours on Lytham Road, for which the organisers paid the princely sum of £5! In the afternoon, we boarded 49 at Marton depot and travelled to Cabin from which I drove it to Gynn Square. Here we used the power-points, turning left and travelling up Dickson Road to North Station. By this time the terminus had been moved, complete with the trolley-reverser outside the Odeon Cinema, and so 49 used it and then went to reverse on the new crossover at Wilton Parade. It returned to Marton via Royal Oak and completed a successful variety of tours during the weekend. The impending demise of the Squires Gate route on Sunday 29th October led Keith Terry to hire Standard 40. To add a tone of piquancy to his tour booking forms: "On tours 1, 2, 3 the cars will be making unique journeys to places where they will never go again". It is true that AKT must be awarded the honour of operating Standard 40 at 4.30pm, as the final tram along Squires Gate Lane.

Talbot Square on the last day of Marton trams, with 48 showing LAYTON on its indicator, and the tour organiser calling to the photographer. *(Maurice Marshall)*

The demise of the Marton route in 1962 resulted in an even greater flurry of activity. A unique tour was held on 29th July 1962 when Marton Vambac 11 was hired for a trip to Fleetwood, the first time to be seen there! This provided an opportunity to picture 11 with a Coronation at the Ferry and at its wartime location at Rossall siding. Gliding up Dickson Road and using the trolley reverser at North Station made it look superior to the Brush cars. In due course, trams fans flocked into the town on 28th October to ride on what had become "Britain's last all-street tramway". In recognition of Marton's trams in the affection of its residents, the Council planned to run a last tram procession from the town centre to Marton. Local fans staged a Tramway Exhibition at the Revoe Library on Central Drive – a former tram route – and there were at least four tours round the route during the day. When the end came, the Transport Department replaced single-deck Marton Vambac cars with Standard 48 to Royal Oak and 40 to Talbot Square. Since I was on a well-

The two cars numbered 40, former B&F Box Car and Corporation Balcony Standard models respectively, which Mr Franklin was offering to the TMS. *(Author)*

filled 48 to Royal Oak, I can never forget the speed at which we returned along Waterloo Road and alarmingly took the curve at Spen corner. When 48 arrived at the depot a large crowd had gathered which we joined, watched it reverse and then disappear inside. At Talbot Square 40 was joined by illuminated Standards 158 and 159 with the official party, and so they travelled impressively past the famous locations – like Winter Gardens and Hippodrome – and arrived outside Marton depot. As each passed through the open green doors there were cheers and flickering of flash bulbs. Afterwards, we local enthusiasts were told by a passing Blackpool Transport official: "Marton has now become NOTRAM!"

Barely had the excitement died down when a bombshell hit the enthusiasts world. A letter to the Tramway Museum Society from Mr JC Franklin on behalf of the Transport Committee, offered the four restored cars 1, 2, 40 and 59, Standards 40 and 49, Railcoach 200 or 208 and a Marton Vambac for preservation. However, any car chosen must be removed from Blackpool by the end of January 1963. The generosity of the offer was swamped by the enormity of the task in hand, and the TMS published the Blackpool Crisis issue of its Journal, appealing for sponsors to raise money for moving and housing the trams at Crich. It was estimated that the price would be £350 per tram and if seven were to be selected, the cost would reach £2,450! It came at a bad time for the TMS, when resources were fully stretched to accommodate seven of the Glasgow cars just after its closure. The urgency from the Transport Department's point of view arose from the closure of Marton and Copse Road depots. Even with the re-opening of Blundell Street depot to trams in March 1963, there would be difficulty in housing all the remaining cars, since half of the building was used as an ambulance station! All volunteers – including myself – circulated appeals for each of the trams, although 49 was bought by Dennis Waters and had arrived at Crich in December 1962. Fortunately, we did succeed in 1963!

Accordingly, the most unseasonal tours in history were organised on 12th and 13th January 1963, when enthusiasts journeyed from all parts of the country to enjoy a last ride on the veterans. That weekend proved to be one of the coldest on record. All who took part will recall the thick hoar frost which clung to everything including the white sleepers, crunched under the feet and gave you numb fingers while trying to manipulate cameras for posterity. Keith Terry was once more in charge of the tours and arranged a bizarre combination of cars to traverse the remaining track. The first tour, using the two 40s was noteworthy for Standard 40's inability to get round the Pleasure Beach loop with spinning wheels and Box 40's frequent dewirements. Sunday morning found your author trudging down the Promenade through the freezing fog, past the partly-completed Lewis's store and seeing ice floating on the sea, just as the historic little No. 1 was emerging spectre-like from the mist. Behind it was Box 40, and the unlikely pair reversed at the Tower to collect the tour party at the Colwyn Hotel on South Promenade. The lights on the top-deck flickered as the car bounced its nautical way along the sinking track, and the future looked as bleak as the weather. We arrived to a huge reception from a crowd armed with a battery of cameras. Keith Terry mounted the top deck to preach to the multitude: "This time there are no restrictions on sitting upstairs and the hardy folk can take full advantage!" We made our way north, Box 40 leading and showing swift progress in many hands. Your author eagerly grasped the controls and got the feel of power as the white sleepers were quickly consumed beneath. At Thornton Gate the cars stopped for photographs and by this time the top-deck passengers and the driver looked ghostly-white. Geoffrey Claydon remarked to the organiser: "Keith, your hair has turned white!" So it was with all who were rash enough to ride on the top-deck of the car. On the way back, sitting in the cosy little saloon of 1, we cast our appreciative eyes round the shining varnished interior and the delightful little blue quarter-lights with their etched star pattern, as if from Bethlehem! The afternoon tour used Dreadnought 59 and Crossbench 2 for a visit to North Station, followed by the finale at the Tower, where Marton Vambac 11 was waiting to take over from 2. This was a fast run down South Promenade, with a stop at Harrowside to record 59 and 11 together in the sun. Vambac 11 had been specially extracted from Marton depot for the tour and travelled along the deserted track in Whitegate Drive and Church Street, fortunately never to return. Subsequently, it went to Hayling Island for a prospective light-rail scheme and then found a home at the East Anglia Transport Museum at Carlton Colville, where it was once again used in active service until 1982. Recently, 11 has been completely restored: its Vambac equipment overhauled, rewired, body rebuilt and repainted in its original post-war livery. Thus, at Easter 2005 Marton Vambac 11 was launched for service again, attractive in appearance and appropriately operating with Standard 159.

On the last day of the North Station route – 27th October 1963 – 59 is demonstrating the use of the trolley-reverser, especially for the photographers including the Author! *(Peter Fitton)*

An embarrassing moment – and a unique event – at Thornton Gate, as Engineering car 3 arrives to rescue derailed 160 from the siding for the passengers' tour once again! *(Dennis Gill)*

However, sad scenes of devastation were enacted in Marton depot, and the once handsome fleet was reduced to scrap metal during March and April 1963. Meanwhile, rumours circulated that a new vehicle museum was to be established at Copse Road depot in Fleetwood. Although vacated in January and the stock of rails and pointwork transferred to Thornton Gate, the depot had been left intact pending a decision about the Museum. The concept was exciting with the Historic Commercial Vehicle Club organising a collection of road and rail vehicles, including trams which would be able to operate in the yard. On 18th March an impromptu procession comprising Tramroad cars 2 and 40 and Standards 40 and 147 travelled up to Copse Road and were driven across the overgrown pointwork to be shut safely inside the depot. Here they stayed while negotiations dragged on and finally collapsed. The only good thing was the extra time that it gave the TMS to prepare for the cars arrival at Crich. The Fleetwood Crossbench car arrived towards the end of September, and the two 40s on 5th October. The single-deck car was delivered on a flat truck, while Standard 40 came on board a Queen Mary trailer, through the winding lanes leading up to Crich Quarry, which was to become their new home. A crane was hired to lift the cars on to their bogies, and a tense moment came when Box 40 was caught by the wind, swung round and caught the crane jib, with an alarmed Keith Pearson on board. However, the two cars were mounted on their trucks by the end of the day, and were shunted along the newly-laid single main line and into one of the new Atcost concrete depots. Crossbench 2 had the honour of becoming the first car to operate under its own power at the Museum on 6th June 1964, going into service on 4th July and carrying members of the public once again, which it still does to this day. Box 40 joined it in service but derailed several times and so was stored at Clay Cross. Subsequently, it went to Heaton Park,Manchester, where it was restored by a working party. It duly returned to Blackpool on 14th June 1988 for the Tramroad 90th Anniversary. Having been stored at Clay Cross again, it reappeared at Blackpool in 1996, where it was restored ready for the Tramroad Centenary in 1998 and will remain in Blackpool until 2010.

The demise of the North Station route on 27th October 1963 was a much more low key affair, since it involved only the abandonment of the track in Dickson Road, the last of Blackpool's street routes. By the final weekend of operation, Service 1 was reduced to a 12-minute headway to Fleetwood, by a collection of shabby Railcoaches and Brush cars. Bispham depot was to be closed as a running shed, and the night cleaners had been transferred to Rigby Road depot before the closure, hence the condition of the cars. Now that the historic cars had departed – No. 1 had been loaned to the British Transport Museum at Clapham – the tour organisers had to apply their ingenuity to stimulate some interest in the event! By this time, the Transport Department were less well disposed towards enthusiasts and tour charges had risen sharply. Hence Keith

Terry had to apologise for the price of 3/6d on his tour by unique Balloon 237 in its all-cream livery. Attempts by the BFTHA to get the new control-trailer set 281-T1 up to North Station was defeated by Mr JC Franklin: "I do not wish a trailer-set to operate on the North Station route." In the event we had to commence on Saturday morning with a tour on Boat 225, which was unique in travelling from Bispham depot along Red Bank Road. Here we found that the depot doors were completely closed, to keep enthusiasts out. On Sunday we used Standard 160, which still remained as a reserve car to the illuminated 158 and 159. It was during this tour that the derailment – now well established in folklore – took place at Thornton Gate. 160 had been to Fleetwood and was bound for North Station when it was suggested that it would make an interesting diversion to explore Thornton Gate sidings. Your author did not need much persuasion, especially since 160 was being followed by Coronation 322 bound for Starr Gate. Thus, the fully loaded Standard inched forward on to the siding and with a sickening lurch dropped down firmly between the rails. The leading wheels were off and the car stood at a drunken angle with no prospects of proceeding, and so everyone evacuated the car and took souvenir pictures. A message was sent with the driver of the Coronation to the Inspector at Cleveleys, who arrived by service car and said: "Now you've done it!" The breakdown van and Engineering car 3 arrived, followed by Chief Engineer Eric Kay who was not amused. However, the fans were treated to a demonstration of re-railing 160. Unfortunately, the lifeguard was broken at the leading end, and consequently 160 had to return to Rigby Road depot with its subdued passengers missing the scheduled visits to North Station and Bispham depot. Subsequently, an irate Mr Franklin wanted to know what a Standard loaded with enthusiasts was doing on the permanent-way siding, and I had some explaining to do. However, I did get the last laugh when, some weeks later, Engineering car 3 derailed at the same place. Thus, the track was found wide of gauge and was quickly relaid! On the same day, during the afternoon tour on Dreadnought 59, it was delightful to observe it using the Odeon trolley-reverser from the top deck. Also, we saw an immaculate Brush car 290 at Bispham Station, waiting to take over the final duties as the last car from North Station to Fleetwood. Two Balloons, 255 and 256, with the official party, followed 290 along Dickson Road and turned back at the Cabin for a reception at the Transport Office. Enthusiasts filled 290 and were finally allowed to ride down Red Bank Road to the depot, being the only group who watched the last car enter Bispham depot. The lights were switched off for the last time and so another chapter had ended.

After all the excitement of those years, the later sixties seemed an anticlimax. Many fans absorbed themselves in the work of establishing a working tramway at Crich, while others – like myself – ventured overseas to experience riding on trams abroad. In March 1965 came the final tour on Dreadnought 59, which had been the Daily Mirror tram each year, and now was due to depart for Crich. Undoubtedly, it was a nostalgic occasion, thinking that we would never see it at Blackpool again, although it did return in 1975! In

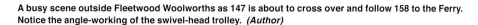

A busy scene outside Fleetwood Woolworths as 147 is about to cross over and follow 158 to the Ferry. Notice the angle-working of the swivel-head trolley. *(Author)*

1966 only three Standards remained, and being hand-braked cars were usually driven by experienced drivers from the former Marton route who could handle them in the crowds on the Promenade. Sadly, this was to be their last year, only 147, 158 and 159 remained and they were designed for museums. Consequently, I remember organising the final Standard tour on 29th October, using 147 and 158 which were well filled and driven by the Chief Engineer Alan Williams. We first travelled to Fleetwood and were able to reverse at Ash Street outside Woolworths, with the trolley's angle-working and watched by devoted enthusiasts. Undoubtedly, this was thought to be a finale of historic cars at Blackpool, and towards the end of the afternoon 158 finally put its lights on. Back at the depot, enthusiasts put coins on the track in order for 147 to create souvenirs of the occasion. So ended traditional tours in the sixties, but things in the future were to change after all!

Following the bleak interlude with the loss of the historic trams during the sixties and culminating in the departure of Standard 147 to Ohio, USA in 1967, a new generation of trams created an interest in tours again. In May 1971, with the foundation of the Fylde Tramway Society by Jack Nichols, their first tour was held on 29th October with OMO 4 in maroon and sunshine-yellow livery, on the day before it went into service on the Fleetwood route. The Light Railway Transport League held its AGM at Blackpool in October 1975, and since it was well attended three cars were used, including two Balloons, 707 and 708, and OMO 5, newly painted in a more striking red-and-cream livery. In contrast, 707 was the first Balloon to be in advertising livery, featuring the local Empire Pools. On the return of Dreadnought 59 in 1975 it was displayed on the promenade opposite the Foxhall hotel. It was then refurbished by the local College of Technology for the Borough Centenary in the following year. This enabled the FTS to have a tour on 59 in June 1978 – the first of many. In November of the same year the launching of a new book, 'Blackpool By Tram' by its authors, gave local enthusiasts an opportunity for a free ride on 59. However, returning via Foxhall Square, 59 split the points and derailed, thus standing in the carriageway. On another tour with 59, I remember it derailing at the St Stephens Avenue stop and it re-railing again while in motion, thanks to the full-passenger load and the paving!

Much excitement for tours focused on the creation of a new Jubilee double-decker, 761, in 1979. The FTS staged a first tour by 761 on 8th July 1979 and it was driven by its Chairman, Jim Ingham, being a regular driver for Blackpool Transport. Later in the year the national LRTL held a tour in somewhat stormy weather, using contrasting 761 and Dreadnought 59. Since track was being relaid in South Shore, the tour from Starr Gate had to travel in reverse round the Pleasure Beach loop in order to gain the southbound track and travel north to Waterloo Road crossover. In the windy storm 59 lost its trolley while on the loop and its rope was seized by an Inspector who replaced it. 1981 saw the arrival of the restored Bolton 66, which was to be

The LRTA party are setting sail on Boat 603, while 708 and OMO 5 wait alongside the Works Fitting Shop for their next tour. *(Author)*

(Above) Enthusiasts capturing the scene at Rossall, as the Western Train makes its first visit there in 1982. *(Author)*

(Below) A delightful scene of 59 posing in front of the Transport Office and Blundell Street Depot, being captured by FTS fans in May 1982. *(Author)*

operated on the Promenade during the Season, carrying fare-paying passengers. This unique agreement between the Bolton 66 Tramcar Trust – who rebuilt the car at Back o' the Bank Power Station – and the Transport Department, augured well for the Centenary celebrations in 1985. The inaugural tour on 66 took place in August by its supporters and on a sunny day provided the great experience of riding a Bolton tram for the first time in Blackpool. Car 66 provided a striking sight travelling round the system in maroon-and-cream lined livery with BOLTON CORPORATION TRAMWAYS and the coat-of-arms making it contrast with the Blackpool fleet. However, March 1982 saw the departure of illuminated Blackpool Belle for Glenwood Trolley Park in USA, and therefore a final tour was held along the Promenade before it went.

The 'eighties became the climax of the tram tours with the Centenary of Promenade tramway in 1985. However the FTS established a new tradition by having a New Year tour on 2nd January 1982 using Coronation 660 with the saloons decorated. The tour started by travelling down Blundell Street and losing its trolley on the curve into Princess Street. Undoubtedly, it was memorable for the flashing wheels, which were making minimal contact because the grooves were full of sand. Some of the passengers were getting a shock as they gripped the handrails because they completed the circuit of the electricity supply. Then followed the journey to Fleetwood with a buffet on the large centre platform. As 1982 would see the demolition of the Blundell Street tram depot, the tours in May, using the Western Train 733/4 and Dreadnought 59, posed the trams in the Rigby Road entrance to the traditional building for the record. The Western Train's journey to Fleetwood provided quite a sensation, because it had not been there before. It reversed on the crossover at

The first 'Tram Sunday' in 1985 included the two Scottish cars – Edinburgh 35 and Glasgow Cunarder 1297 – operating between the Ferry and Ash Street. *(Author)*

North Albert Street and travelled with the carriage first to Ash Street, where it then travelled to the Ferry in the conventional way. Undoubtedly local people shopping in Lord Street stared at this unusual spectacle! Photographic stops in tours always provided opportunity to capture the trams on interesting settings and so the former Rossall siding saw 733 and 734 there. In 1983 Blackpool Transport commenced a Vintage Tour, using Bolton 66 and a Ribble Leyland Lion bus. With the FTS trying it first, we travelled to Knott End via Poulton-le-Fylde, then crossed the river Wyre to Fleetwood by ferry where we boarded Bolton 66 to return to Blackpool. At the end of the year the Christmas Festival was celebrated by using Rocket 732, which was a somewhat uncomfortable location for the buffet. On our return from Fleetwood Ferry, as the organiser I was told that Keith Terry was missing, perhaps left behind. When we arrived at Rossall for photographs he emerged from the driver's cab, having possibly driven the Rocket there. I wasn't too surprised!

On 19th November 1983 Edinburgh 35 became the first of the visiting trams for the Centenary, and on Good Friday 1984, it appeared on a Promenade tour for the National Savings employees whose department had sponsored it. The sight of this car in maroon-and-white livery, reminded enthusiasts that it had been preserved in Shrubhill Works after the closure of the City tramway in 1956, and now it was operating at Blackpool. Glasgow Cunarder 1297 arrived from the National Tramway Museum on 5th April, through picturesque St Michaels-on-Wyre. At first fitted with a pantograph for a trial run, 1297 lost the overhead on the Ferry curves and had to be towed back. Then it was fitted with a trolley and journeyed successfully to Fleetwood on 24th April, proving it was ready for future tours. A tour with a trio of historic trams – 35, 1297 and 66 – followed, first running to South Shore and then north, with the Scottish trams leaving Bolton 66 behind. They waited on Little Bispham loop for 66 to join them, but unfortunately it derailed on the points there. Many pictures were taken by the crowd of enthusiasts, with the service cars having to temporarily work on a single line. To continue the tour, all the passengers had to crowd on the two remaining trams, which reversed and journeyed north to Cleveleys. I remember filming fully loaded 1297 and 35 at Rossall, proceeding rapidly and confirming the reputation of speedy trams in large cities!

On 21st October it was possible to use the new Centenary 641 with Coronation 660, the former having arrived from East Lancs Coachbuilders on 17th April. The tour on 21st October was interesting in comparing two trams of a different generation. While similar in size, 641 was 51ft 6ins in length and rather square in shape, compared with the curvaceous shape of the Coronation. When I rode on the two cars alternately, in order to evaluate the riding qualities, it was clear that there was a difference. The Coronation maintained a smooth riding quality while bouncing on its bogie-springs when crossing pointwork. On the other hand 641 was prone to rolling from side to side, owing to the Metalastik suspension of its bogies. In the respective saloons, it was clear that Coronation 660 was more spacious and brighter, while 641 was more compact with passenger flow but had front saloon seats facing backwards. Next, Sheffield 513 arrived from Beamish on 24th October, and the FTS hired it for their festive 1984 tour. This was its first passenger journey here, where it looked very appropriate in local Fleetwood streets, reminiscent of its operation in Sheffield until 1960. I do remember how the riding was more nautical, since 513 bounced on a 4-wheel truck. A representative from Beamish suggested that it should slow down on the reserved track to prevent derailing. Sure enough, many years later, 513 did indeed derail, confirming their advice!

The Centenary year of 1985 undoubtedly provided the most rewarding opportunity to have tours on such a variety of trams originating from many different cities. By the FTS Convention weekend on 4-6th May, Balloon 706 had been restored to its original open-top condition and so its first tour was momentous for the 70 passengers. While experiencing the ride on an open-top Balloon for the first time – apart from the older generation – we did have some reservations about its pantograph and the short roof necessary to shield passengers from it. On the following day, Dreadnought 59 was joined by Standard 40 – having returned from NTM on 26th April – and the two in the same red-and-white livery made a magnificent sight. During the same weekend Sheffield 513 and Coronation 660 – both having been built by Roberts of Wakefield – provided a memorable tour. While they are entirely different in size, their appearance in cream-coloured bodies provide similarities and yet differing riding qualities. Pantograph 167 arrived in May from Bolton, where it had been restored by Derek Shepherd's team. In the same month Manchester Californian car 765 came from Heaton Park in exchange for Boat 600. Cars 167 and 765 made a joint tour on 11th May. Organised by Tram Sponsorship Organisation – sponsor of 167 – the tour made it possible to ride on contrasting types, with 167 as a saloon car of 1928 and 765 of 1914 with unvestibuled front and open side facing wooden seats.

An opportunity to ride on all these historic cars in Fleetwood took place on 14th July – which became known as 'Tram Sunday' – and the sight of them shuttling between the Ferry and Ash Street provided entertainment for the general public. Before the Centenary Day of 29th September, Hill of Howth open-topper 10 – with its gauge changed from 5ft 3in – was welcomed by Joanna Lumley at North Pier, before she later switched on the Illuminations. On the day before the Centenary procession, a tour on Howth 10 was held, and its open top-deck provided an ideal location for viewing of all the historic cars operating that day. One of the great advantages of a tour on 10 was the high railings round the upper-deck, thus permitting standing passengers, and, in the saloon, longitudinal back-to-back central seating enabled passengers to sit facing out. On the following day the weather remained good and the 20 trams in the procession left the depot loaded with passengers, many from the tram's original location or the Museum Societies. The procession from North Pier to the Pleasure Beach, along the original conduit line, was led by Conduit car 4 powered by batteries and carrying official guests dressed in Victorian costumes. Crowds of thousands watched the procession and were amazed when the final one proved to be steam-engine 'John Bull' of 1885, made in Manchester and built for New South Wales. During the rest of the day, historic trams were operated along the line, providing a clear reason why it was the most popular tram-riding day in Blackpool's 100 year tramway history.

At the end of 1985, the finale with two trams from the National Tramway Museum – 1885 Conduit car 4 and Standard 40 – provided a unique occasion. Passengers on 4 were dressed in 19th century costumes which seemed appropriate for the journey along the original Princess Street line. The two cars then went to Starr Gate and along the Promenade to the Tower, at the slow speed determined by the batteries powering the eye-catching diminutive open-topper.

Without question 706 looked a handsome open-topper in 1985, even if it had the single indicator and pantograph. Number 167 is following, with Manchester 765 on the siding. *(Author)*

The most memorable Topless Tour featured Dreadnought 59, Howth 10 and 706, seen here at Starr Gate before their journey to Fleetwood. *(Author)*

The weather held and, being a sunny day, the sight of the 1885 car running for the final time at Blackpool made a nostalgic sight with the Tower. Since then it has been on static exhibition at Crich NTM, but since 2005, on special occasions, 4 has been seen running once again at Crich.

A memorable tour in 1987 was Keith Terry's 'Topless Tour', with three open-toppers – Howth l0, Dreadnought 59 and Balloon 706 – making a fine sight and varied experience for the passengers. In the following year the Glasgow Garden Festival event took place and Blackpool sent Boat 606, painted blue and yellow, along with Edinburgh 35 and Crich sent Glasgow 22, 68 and 1297 to take part. This was a new line laid in Govan alongside the River Clyde, and provided the first opportunity to catch a tram in that city since its tramway finished in September 1962. The compensation for Blackpool was the return of Box saloon 40, having been restored in Manchester's Heaton Park where it had also been operated.

A busy moment in Lord Street, Fleetwood during the tour, with Tramroad saloon 40 and open-top Dreadnought 59 passing each other on the May 1990 tour. *(Author)*

An historic scene at Fleetwood Ferry on 16th July 1998, with the three cars – B & F Crossbench 2, B & F Box 40 and Pantograph 167 – finally together. *(Author)*

Tramroad Centenary

Celebrating the 90th Anniversary of the Blackpool & Fleetwood Tramroad, Box 40 made a tour to Fleetwood on 16th July. It would be 25 years since some of us had taken such a traditional ride over the Tramroad on 40, along with Conduit 4. With its long wheelbase, 40 gave a good ride over the sleeper-track and being high-riding was ideal for good sightseeing on a tour. Large advertising panels were fitted between its bogies for Fisherman's Friend, who had sponsored the restoration and return of the tram. However, further improvements were made in February 1989, when its seats were covered with new tartan moquette. In that year, a new tour in August featured Brush car 636, painted in the wartime green livery with cream flares. On this occasion, driver Philip Higgs was wearing an appropriate tin hat and carrying a gas mask. On 21st October, Howth 10 made its final tour of Blackpool before returning to Crich. It had certainly been an eye-catcher, and provided an experience of the Dublin Hill of Howth line which closed in 1959. So, by the end of the decade, Blackpool had lost some of the interesting trams which had been there for the Centenary. The year ended with Coronation 660 in use for the FTS Christmas tour, involving a change to a bus at Ash Street – because of the track-relaying under way in North Albert Street.

In May 1990, the annual FTS Convention weekend featured Box 40 and Dreadnought 59 seen together for the last time. Since they had originally belonged to different fleets, 40 being an inter-urban saloon and 59 a Promenade open-topper, they were painted in contrasting liveries. While they provided differing experiences, their passage along Lord Street, Fleetwood was captured for posterity. The final tour on 59 was held on 11th November, before it departed for Crich. Many of the participants sought to handle its controls, safely under the guidance of the driver, while on the reserved tracks. This had been one of the traditions of Blackpool tram tours, adding much enjoyment, but which was subsequently prevented from happening.

The Dreadnought was first on display in the exhibition hall at Crich, but was later moved to Clay Cross store and has remained there ever since. Considering that it was an attraction in Blackpool for 16 years, it seems high time it was restored to working order. The 'nineties decade continued with tram tours, and the

(Above) Crossbench car 2 raised off the track, with pairs of its wheels in the foreground without the motors.

(Centre) New grooved boards have been fitted, and new canvas applied to the raised centre section of the roof. Seats and body-frame have been varnished.

(Below) The new underframe is completed ready for fitting. Notice the frame shape with wooden cross members and bogie bolster mountings.
(DM Bearsdell all)

forthcoming Centenary of the Blackpool & Fleetwood Tramroad, in 1998, provided the perfect reason to arrange the return of historic trams. First to return was Box 40 on 23rd April 1996 and in June it was fully repainted and enhanced with gold lettering of BLACKPOOL & FLEETWOOD TRAMROAD together with CENTENARY 1898 – 1998. This had been financed by 'Friends of 40' along with Fleetwood Tram Sunday Committee and the North Euston Hotel, who were credited on the display boards.

Next was the arrival of Stockport 5, handed over by Stan Heaton, who had inaugurated its restoration. At Fleetwood Tram Sunday it led the procession but was not allowed to carry the public and was then returned to the depot. It subsequently had to be fitted with air brakes and approved by the Railway Inspector, following which it toured for its working party from Salford Mode Wheel on 17th May 1998. The 'Friends of 40' enjoyed their first tour on 10th August 1996, especially stopping for photographs in Rossall fields, where the Tramroad line maintains its original appearance. Before the Centenary Year, open-top Marton Box 31 arrived back on 10th September 1997, its top-deck railings having caught in tree branches while en-route from Beamish. Looking very smart in the red-and-white livery, it was last seen in Blackpool on 17th July 1984 – as a grubby green works car 754 – what a transformation from its native tramway!

Fortunately, the occasion of a Centenary activates the restoring of historic trams, and so it was not surprising that Box 40 was ready in good time, and 1898 Crossbench car 2 with 1928 Pantograph 167 were to follow from Crich. In November of the previous year the bogies of 2 were dismantled, cleaned and painted, and the GE-1000 motors were sent away for the wearing on the armature bearings to be examined. At the same time the roof canvas was removed to repair the planking. When the floor was removed it was found that extensive rot on the underframe indicated the requirement for a completely new frame to be made. All this was taking place in the workshop at Crich, while other developments were taking place at Blackpool. Boat 600 returned from Heaton Park and was fitted with new windscreens and completely repainted in its original livery, complete with Municipal coat-of-arms.

In May 1998, a notable first tour was held for 'Friends of Stockport 5', and their car travelled round the system including a ride to Fleetwood. It made a striking sight, as a small open-topper in red-and-white livery with a 4-wheel truck. Riding on the open top-deck made a memorable experience, as 5 bounced over pointwork and rail joints on the deteriorating Fleetwood track, so that the wooden seats could drop away

Stockport 5 looking smart at Fleetwood Ferry on 17th May 1998 during its first visit. *(Author)*

Crossbench 2 on the Centenary journey to Fleetwood on 1st July 1998, passing the Metropole Hotel on the street track, and with the Tower in view. *(Peter Fitton)*

and return with considerable force beneath you. Fortunately, the tours on the FTS Convention, using Boat 600 and Balloon 706, did not produce the same experience, since bogie cars gave a more comfortable ride.

At Crich, restoration of Crossbench car 2 was proceeding apace, including re-varnishing of the seats and painting of the body-frame. After repainting the Pantograph car 167, the work culminated in trial runs at Crich on 21st June. On the following day the trams arrived in Blackpool, were unloaded and 2 was driven towards the depot having not been seen there since 1963. Sadly, numbers 2 and 167 were to stay for only three weeks, during which time they had to mark historic occasions as well as carry out tours.

These began with the depot open day on Sunday 28th June, when there was a fine display of historic trams and a Circular tour from the depot to the Tower which returned via Princess and Blundell Streets. Clearly this was a memorable occasion for enthusiasts, especially when riding on Marton 31 when it twice derailed on the curve near to the original depot. It was replaced by Bolton 66, which did not derail there, although Boats 600 and 607 were inclined to do so. Finally in that afternoon, it was decided to use twin-car 675/685 for the first time on the Circular tour, but 675 did derail on the curve as witnessed by local residents and fascinated enthusiasts. There followed the commemoration of the first tram to Fleetwood on 1st July, using Tramroad cars 2 of 1898 and 40 of 1914. This was filmed by a television crew, and the trams were cheered by school children at most of the Tramroad stations. At Ash Street, Fleetwood, a large crowd of pupils from Chaucer Road school greeted them by waving flags and cheering, as their predecessors did in 1898. On two Saturdays, 4th and 11th July, the three historic cars were used on a continuous shuttle-service between Cleveleys and Fleetwood, for members of TMS & FTS who had supported the cost of their return. They certainly experienced unique rides on 2 and 40, recalling Tramroad days before 1920 and also the operation of 167 from 1928 to 1960. Riding on the crossbench seats of 2 provided an opportunity to get the feel of early Company days along the Tramroad. The repeated passage of 2, 40 and 167 along Fleetwood streets provided an unusual sight for the populace. They were keen to have a ride on them, but RESERVED on the indicators of 40 and 167 showed they were only on tour. Centenary Day on 12th July, with a procession led by 2 and 619, 40, 167 from the Pleasure Beach to Fleetwood Ferry, was accompanied by gale force wind and rain which kept away the crowds seen previously in 1985. However, Tram Sunday had better weather, with 167, Box 40, Marton 31, Bolton 66, Vanguard 619 and Balloon 706 giving rides between the Ferry and Ash Street. On the previous day, the FTS held a final tour on 167 and 31, when they made a splendid sight, being of different types and liveries. The absence of 1898 Crossbench car 2 from such events seems to have indicated concern about its safety amongst crowds of people, since the running boards along the side were easy to mount and fall off, especially these days! The Centenary occasion had shown how these trams originally operated and it is hoped to repeat the exercise for the 125th Anniversary of the promenade tramway in 2010.

Enthusiasts always enjoy riding by tram along the Fylde coast, as long as types are frequently changed to stimulate their support and Annual tours always take place, at New Year by the 'Friends of 40' and on Bolton 66 to Fleetwood in spring, and a tour of the Illuminations in the autumn, for its supporters.

However, the year 2000 was notable for the departure of Boat 606 for Trolleyville, USA in exchange for Standard 147. On its last day of operation in Blackpool, 606 was seen on the Promenade without its windscreens. Well-known tram enthusiasts Chris Pulling and Graham Twidale subsequently took it to Fleetwood as an exclusive tour. Being in the liaison team, these two saw it arrive at Trolleyville where it immediately operated for the enthusiasts there. The most striking return to Blackpool was thus that of 147 on Wednesday 18th October, but it had been neglected and disused at Trolleyville, and had become a home for racoons. The trio from Blackpool – including Mike Airey of Blackpool Transport – had hosed it down and separated its upper and lower saloons for transportation. Having landed at Seaforth and been transported to Blackpool, upon arrival at Rigby Road 147 was assembled on the bus park and shunted into track 2 of the depot. This reminded me that I had organised its last tour in 1966.

While work on 147 proceeded in the Fitting and Body Shops during the winter, on 15th February Sheffield 513 returned here from Beamish, being too modern to fit in there. On 29th August 2001, an inaugural run was made to Fleetwood for 633, rebuilt in the shape of former trawler 'Cevic FD 142'. The Lofthouse family, who had sponsored the new illuminated car to advertise Fisherman's Friend, were taken for a ride between the Ferry and Ash Street. It looked very impressive with high bows, red-and-white bulbs outlining its profile, and its white superstructure lit from inside. The FTS naturally used it for their Christmas tour that year, along with contrasting Coronation 660.

On 17th September 2001 there was a presentation of cheques towards the restoration of 147 to the departing Managing Director, Tony Depledge, by Fylde Tramway Society and 'Friends of 40'. Accordingly, 147 was towed out of the Fitting Shop and it was now in the traditional livery. Soon all the details had been completed, including the brass handrails, fitting the missing quarterlights, and new ruby moquette cushions for the saloon seats. Gold lining and numerals completed its appearance, along with a plaque on the saloon partition listing those who had contributed to its restoration. This paid a tribute to all those fans who were keen to see 147 again at Blackpool and had financially helped the scheme.

Standard 147 was launched on 3rd April 2002, although I have to admit that I first saw it at Cleveleys Square on 28th March, making a trial trip to Fleetwood. It looked beautiful in its traditional livery and was perfect in its performance as it passed through Rossall fields and down Lord Street. On the day of its launch, many invited guests assembled in the Pleasure Beach Casino and watched 147 arrive, turn on the loop-line before we joined it to travel to North Pier. Here a ceremony was performed by Joan Humble MP who unveiled the dash, this being filmed for television news. The journey to Fleetwood was rewarding over the newly relaid track between Norbreck and Little Bispham, and it arrived at the Ferry showing ROYAL OAK on its indicators. The last tour on 147 took place 36 years previously, but on that occasion it did not have such gleaming woodwork, whereas now it represents a fine tradition of Blackpool Standard Tramcars.

On 9th June another welcome arrival was marked by the return of Coronation 304, sponsored by the Channel 4 television programme *Salvage Squad*, which showed the tram's restoration in one of a series of such programmes – though only this one involved a tramcar. In this case, it made possible the Lancastrian Transport Trust's dream, for they had owned the car for some years and had attempted to restore it in St Helens transport museum, alongside many buses. The grant of £25,000 made it a reality and provided the programme's viewers with an interesting subject, appropriately chosen because its name reflected the 50th anniversary of the Queen's Coronation in 1953. LTT was given a fenced compound in the rear corner of the depot where work could proceed, including rewiring, repanelling, refitting sliding windows and so on by tram fans, some of whom had professional skills. While it made an interesting television programme in 2002, its first actual appearance was filmed on 6th January 2003 whilst driven by Philip Higgs. On a bright and sunny day the ride between the Tower and the Pleasure Beach provided a big thrill for its supporters and those who recorded it. Not generally realised was the fact that 304 had to be driven on crawling-notches rather than using the full output of the Vambac equipment, since it was by then realised that it had been on fire in the past. Bowers of Derby came to collect the Vambac equipment in March and constructed a new frame to replace the one made of Bakelite. This seems to have been one of the original Achilles heel's of the equipment and another reason why Vambacs were phased out.

On 12th April 2003, once the track laying had been completed by Birse Group on several sections of the line, the Fleetwood tram service was reinstated north of Thornton Gate. Unfortunately, double-decker trams were not allowed to operate until the whole section of the line between Thornton Gate and Fisherman's Walk was completed during the following winter. Consequently, for the first time in history, the service was operated by twin cars, although they were known as 'elephants' by the staff, since they were slow and

(Above) Newly-restored Standard 147 and Railcoach 679 repainted in the 'eighties livery, contrast with each other on the FTS tour, 3rd May 2004.

(Below) A 2004 Christmas tour for FTS using two illuminated cars: 736 Frigate and 633 Trawler 'Cevic', seen here at Harrowside. *(Author, both)*

needed more running time. On Tram Sunday that year the Western Train was displayed at the Ferry and had to be towed there. The saloon trailer was towed by Trawler 633, both of which happened to be sponsored by Fisherman's Friend. Only single-deckers could take part that year and so Box 40, Crossbench 619, Boat 600 and Coronation 660 were used on the historic service to Thornton Gate. Unfortunately, they had fewer passengers than in previous years when, until 1999, they went to the Ferry.

Following some major reconstruction on the Vambac's rotor, where the fire had occurred, it was possible to restore power and motion to the dormant Coronation and the second programme of *Salvage Squad*, featuring the completely restored car, was made on the evening of 11th September, showing it passing through the Illuminations – and travelling at speed. However, the climax came on 8th November that year when the first tour was held using the two preserved Coronations, numbers 304 and 660. This was certainly an historic occasion, since two Coronations had not been seen together for thirty years! They were painted in the traditional livery, with chrome beading at each end, but the great difference was that 660 did not have the

(Above) Coronations 304 and 660 seen together at North Pier on 8th November 2003, for the first time in 30 years, making a truly memorable occasion.

(Below) The two Coronations in Bold Street Fleetwood, a traditional location for service cars including Coronations for 20 years, but now in May 2005 and on tour. *(Author, both)*

Vambac equipment, nor did it have the opening standee windows and the fluorescent lighting. However, they seemed to have exactly the same riding qualities. A series of shuttle tours were held, although on the first northbound journey, 304 broke down and had to be pushed by 660 to Thornton Gate. Fortunately, the problem was soon solved and later in the afternoon the two Coronations went to Fleetwood Ferry and made a striking sight. This was without doubt a great achievement for LTT, who had restored 304 in its native Blackpool, where it is again able to demonstrate an important part of the history of tramcar evolution in the Borough.

By Easter 2004 all of the track north of Thornton Gate had been completely relaid and Balloons returned to service in May until the end of the Illuminations. One delightful aspect was the frequent use of 700, then complete with trolley and wearing the handsome green livery. On Tram Sunday in July 304 was driven to the Ferry, where it stood on display all day, and returned at speed once Lord Street had been cleared of its

(Above) Standard 147 seen again in its traditional location of Princess Street, as though returning to the original Blundell Street depot. While actually giving rides to enthusiasts, this was the depot route for all trams coming back to Hopton Road depot, while Manchester Square junction was being relaid.

(Centre) Coronation 304 in Foxhall Square on its way back to the depot after trial runs on 27th April 2005, prior to a tour with fellow Coronation 660 during May weekend. The Spiv gave rides here in February and certainly looks striking in this traditional location. Notice the trolley-pole controlling the wheel on the overhead.

(Below) Balloon 700 approaching along Princess Street towards Foxhall Square during the historic rides day. In its traditional livery it seems entirely appropriate in such a location. However, there is one mistake, in the form of the hoods over the windscreens. These were removed when the open-toppers were converted to enclosed Balloons during the Second World War.
(Author, all)

exhibits. During the year, work was proceeding on the illuminated frigate HMS Blackpool, No. 736. It was 'launched' on 11th September – perhaps fittingly in a storm – by the Mayor of Blackpool and with guard-of-honour provided by sea cadets outside the Transport Office. With Trawler 633 these two illuminated trams restored the traditional feature to the Illuminations scene, something sadly missed since 2000. The FTS duly had a Christmas tour with 633 and 736, which made it possible to compare the interior saloons and riding qualities. For those fans – like myself – with long memories, the sound of the original Pantograph 170 with its GEC Witton motors could be heard clearly on 736 during the ride! However, one of the most unusual forms of tour took place on 27th February 2005, when the previously disused track in Princess and Blundell Streets was in use for depot access while Manchester Square junction was being relaid. It was called 'By Tram to Foxhall' – using 147, 700, 678 and 304 – riding on each of the trams and capturing them in an historic location. During the previous year, Coronation 660 was restored by repanelling and re-fitting of the winding windows, except for four which had to be replaced by fixed glass. Happily, it was repainted in the traditional livery, with Gill-sans gold numerals on each end, although BTS did not refit the chrome beading. The two Coronations appeared together in May 2005 for the FTS tour and, while slightly different in detail, they made a handsome pair. They confirmed their pedigree in having operated the Fleetwood route for 20 years. Later that year – 15th July – there was another opportunity to share experiences with fellow enthusiasts who enjoy tram riding, share common interests and capture the events for posterity.

There are still more opportunities for special tours on unusual trams as the Western Train, which was built in 1962 from Railcoach 209 and Pantograph car 174, using the spare towing equipment from the ten Twin-cars, is due to see a new lease of life in due course. Seating 94 passengers, it was created in the traditional style of the US steam locomotive and carriage, and was sponsored by ABC Television. Its appearance featured an illuminated cowcatcher, brass bell and smoking funnel, making it the most popular illuminated tram of its time. It was withdrawn in 1999 and seen again for the first time in 2003 on Fleetwood Tram Sunday at the Ferry terminus. There was a strong demand for its restoration and its ability to return to the Illuminations. A grant for £278,000 was given by the Heritage Lottery Fund in 2006 and the work in restoring it to its original appearance will take two years. We look forward to its reappearance with eager anticipation.

I hope that this part of the book has brought to life some of the great tradition of tours in Blackpool, which began in 1938 and continues to this day. Undoubtedly, there will be many who remember some of the more notable excursions and it is, of course, by using such restored historic trams for enjoyment and publicity that we ensure that tram operation will continue to remain one of the four famous Blackpool attractions, the others being, in the Author's opinion, the Tower, the Pleasure Beach and the Golden Mile.

Box 40 in January 2006, newly-repainted with 'BLACKPOOL & FLEETWOOD' added at each end, starting its annual tour of the system for 'Friends of 40' outside the depot. *(Peter Fitton)*

Look Out! Illuminated Trams

TRAMNIK ONE

(Above) The first of the post-war illuminated trams was showboat Blackpool Belle in 1959. It was extremely attractive with cabin windows illuminated at two levels, the funnel concealing the trolley mast and the paddles simulated by fluorescent tubes. Thirty-two passengers sat on four benches facing out, while music was played by equipment in the upper saloons. It was built from Toastrack 163, operated in this form until 1978, then in 1982 was sent to Oregon Trolley Park, USA. Sadly, it has not kept its original attractive appearance. *(Author's Collection)*

(Centre) In 1961 the most unusual illuminated tram took the form of a Space rocket and was called Tramnik One, built on the frame of Pantograph car 168. The driver's cab was beneath the saloon, tilted at 20°, and the rear entrance was between the mock power jets. At the front of the saloon was a cockpit with the two astronauts. It was withdrawn after the 1999 Lights and given to the Lancastrian Transport Trust who arranged its last journey on 28th April 2002. *(Author)*

(Below) Hovertram 735 was built from EE Railcoach 222 in 1963 and carried 99 passengers. Owing to the illuminated engines on the roof, the upper saloon had low-bridge bus seating with a side gangway. Being a double-decker it carried the most seated passengers and its appearance was striking. Eventually, lighting was removed from its rear panels to avoid shocks for passengers boarding by the rear entrance. It ceased operation in 1999 and is currently stored until being rewired and its body completely rebuilt. *(Author's Collection)*

At North Pier, the Western Train and Hovertram wait to take passengers on a Tour of the Illuminations. The two-car assembly is impressive by night and by day as these two photographs show, but with very different appearance – the night certainly has magic! (Author)

Standing at the Fleetwood terminus, a stone's throw away from the ships in the estuary, the sponsorship by Fisherman's Friend seems very real and appropriate. (Peter Fitton)

The first sight of the Western Train since 1999, here at Fleetwood Ferry on Tram Sunday 2003. The public could step on board and see why it needed restoring. Number 733 was sloping down at each end, while the trailer was straight, but its woodwork needs to be reconditioned. When it returned to the depot, trailer 734 was towed by Trawler 633. As can be seen they are both appropriately advertising Fisherman's Friend. *(Author)*

The Trawler at the Ferry on tour in December 2001, showing its striking profile. Built on a new underframe of Brush car 633, it was introduced in September that year, after being inaugurated by the Lofthouse family on 29th August. *(Charlie Parsons)*

(Right) Cevic Trawler 633 loading at North Pier for a Tour in 2006. Notice the correct trawler profile with high bows, winding winch and bridge, and Fisherman's Friend adverts along the sides. Because it can be driven from both ends it has two indicators. *(RP Fergusson)*

(Centre) Stern view of Frigate 736, with the helicopter, a hangar and funnel. The illuminated lines are broken near to the front by an emergency exit. Originally built in 1965 upon the frame of Pantograph 170 and then rebuilt in 2004 with 24 volt AC wiring, and easier access for passengers plus air conditioning. *(Author)*

(Foot) View of the bows with its fleet number, tapered driver's cab with the guns above it, and the bridge. The main entrance is near the stern and the emergency exit is in the foreground. Notice the high mounted controller and the curved windows for upward viewing. *(Author)*

Bolton 66 at Rigby Road before embarking on another Tour of the Lights for its sponsors and friends in 2005. *(John A Senior)*

STANDARDS 1924	40, 41, 48, 49, 147, 158, 159, 160 (scrapped: 41 - 1961, 160 - 1965)	8 now	1
	five are preserved - see list. 158 was dismantled at Crich NTM		
PANTOGRAPHS 1928:	168 - 175 (167 Works-car, 176 redesigned then scrapped 1954)	8 now	0
	168 became Rocket, 170 - Frigate, 174 Western Train carriage.		
RAILCOACH 1933-4:	200 - 224: 20 scrapped 1961 - 1965, Marton Vambac 208,		
	209 Western Train loco 1962, 222 - Hovertram 1963 - 2007.		
	OMO 3 - 224, OMO 4 - 220, OMO 5 - 221 preserved NTM.	25 now	0
OPEN BOATS 1934:	225 - 236 (scrapped 1968: 229, 231, 232, 234) others 600-607	12 now	5
BALLOONS 1934-5:	237 - 263 (700 - 726). 705 scrapped after accident with 706 1982.	27 now	24
	725 & 714 became Jubilee cars 761 & 762 in 1979 & 1982.		2
	700 restored to 1942 style -1997, 717 restored to 1935 style - 2007.		
RAILCOACH 1936:	264 - 283 (611 - 620) became OMOs 1 & 2, 6 - 13 in 1972 - 1976.		
Series 2	272 - 281 (672 - 681) became towing-cars of twin-sets 1960-01	20 now	6
	677 dismantled in 2007 to restore 209 as Western Train.		
	678 - 680 reverted to being single-railcoaches in 1972.	now	3
TRAILERS 1960:	T1 - T10 (681 - 690) built by MCW.	(10 now	7)
	681 - 687 fitted with controllers 1963 - 1970 permanently-coupled.		
	688 scrapped in 1982, 689 & 690 scrapped in Bradford 1989.		
BRUSH-CARS 1937:	284 - 303 (621 - 638), 303 fitted with VAMBAC - scrapped 1963.	20 now	12
	290 became track-trailer in 1973 - 260, 287 towed it as 259 & now		
	preserved by LTT. 298 preserved by N.T.M.; 292, 301, 302 scrapped.		
	633 rebuilt as Trawler Cevic in 2001 and now an illuminated car.		
MARTON-VAMBACS:	10 - 21 built as sun-saloons 1939, re-fitted 1948-9 for Marton.	12 now	0
1939	10 scrapped after collision 1961, 12 - 21 scrapped in depot 1963.		
	11 preserved at EATM Carlton Colville, restored in 2006.		
CORONATIONS	304 - 328 (641 - 664), thirteen fitted with E.E. Z6 controllers:	25 now	1
1952-4	323, 310, 328, 306, 327, 324, 318, 326, 322, 325, 321, 320, 319.		
	313 first scrapped in 1968, followed by Vambacs in 1969 & the		
	others 1971 - 1975. 660 (324) was retained by B.T.S., 304 is		
	preserved and returned for t.v. in 2003. 663 (327) at LTT Marton.		

TOTALS (including twin-cars): 157 now 54

CENTENARY CARS	641 - 648 replaced the OMO cars as principal service-cars.		8
1984-86	648 was 651 with GEC equipment. Three more should have been built.		
VANGUARD 1987:	Built from OMO 7 in 1987 at Mode Wheel in Salford.		1

PRESENT   FLEET   TOTAL: 63

ILLUMINATED CARS:

WESTERN TRAIN:	1962 - 733 & 734 - Railcoach 209 & Pantograph 174 seats 95, restored in 2007.	
FRIGATE:	1965 - 736 - Pantograph 170 - 75 seats, rebuilt in 2004 with new appearance.	
TRAWLER CEVIC:	2001 - 633 - Brush-car is sponsored by Fisherman's Friend, and is dual-ended.	

TOTAL: 3

VINTAGE TRAMS LOANED:

BOLTON 66	1901	Arrived on 23 June 1981 from restoration at Back 0' the Bank Power Station, Bolton. Brill 21E maximum-traction bogies from Belgium.
B & F BOX 40	1914	To Crich NTM October 1963, Heaton Park 1979 - 1988, in Blackpool 1988-91, and again 22 April 1996 for Tramroad Centenary until 2010. Built by UEC Preston, McGuire bogies, 2 x 40 h.p. BTH motors.
STOCKPORT 5	1901	Arrived 28 May 1996 from Salford Mode Wheel, where restored. Brill 21E 4-wheel truck from Oporto 67, Controllers E.E. DB1.
SHEFFIELD 513	1951	Arrived 14 February 2001 from Beamish, and last here in Centenary 1985. Body by Roberts, Maley & Taunton 4-wheel 9ft. truck, 2 x 60 h.p. motors. Allen-West controllers, and Westinghouse air-brakes.
CORONATION 304	1952	Arrived 9 June 2002 after 30 years, sponsored by Channel 4 Salvage Squad for restoration in their programme. Work done in the depot compound, and televised in January 2003 & September 2003.

TOTAL: 5

COMPLETE   TOTAL: 71